LOOK BEYOND
THE SCARS

LOOK BEYOND THE SCARS

CONNIE HANAGAN

To order additional copies of this book, contact:
Xlibris Corporation
1-888-795-4274
www.Xlibris.com
Orders@Xlibris.com
44544

Dedication

To my son James, the greatest gift I have ever received in my life. For your wonderful way of understanding and support throughout not only this book but my life, and for loving me for the person I am. Everyone says I did a great job bringing you up, but I only brought you to your first step, and then watched you walk through life on your own. Being an only child I know was not easy for you, but through it all you made the right choices. James, walk with your head up high because you are a unique person and you have wonderful qualities. James, you will always be my best friend, and for that my love is with you always.

James, 2006

To my mother and father, who have passed through this life. I know that if you were here you would still find it hard to understand, but at least now you would have answers to some questions that were never asked but were just accepted. How hard it must have been for you both to see me in all those hospitals. I am so sorry you had to see me go through my life like that, but I had no control over my self-abuse. You did the best you could. Thank you both for loving me without words.

To my sisters Jane and Mary. Throughout my stays at the hospitals you were there trying your best to understand what I was going through, when no one did, not even myself at that time. I love you both and the closeness we have today. Thank you for all your love, help, and support throughout this book and my life.

To my big brothers Jackie and Jim. Along with the rest of the family they just accepted it, although Jackie used to get mad at me and tell me to stop cutting myself because I was hurting Mom. Believe me if I could have stopped I would have. But I had no control at that time in my life.

To Patty you will always remain in my heart as the younger sister I never had. You have taken so much time from your own busy schedule to always lend me a hand, not only with my book but throughout my life. You were always there for me. Please know that I will always be here for you. I will always love you.

To Katherine, you also will never be forgotten for the time you flew down from MO. and spent a week trying to help me sort out a lot of my errs (because of my dyslexia) it was not easy for me, but you were very patient and helped me with some chapters of my book. And to you my deepest gratitude and warmest thanks.

Dedicated to the finest woman I have ever had the pleasure of knowing.

This is a day in July I will never forget as long as I live; it is the day I lost my best friend, Barbara. Not only was she my best friend, she was the most caring person in the world, as you will read in this newspaper article.

Her nursing went far beyond the call of duty. After we both left the Boston State hospital, her a nurse and I a patient, she made it known to me that I could call her any time and she would be there for me. Nights were much harder for me back then, so if I called Barbara at night where she was working, she would tell me to go to her mother's. Barbara lived with and took care of her mom, and I was very close to both of them. I would meet Barbara there after work, and we would talk for hours; sometimes she let me stay overnight when it got too late. I loved Barbara and her mom very much, and they both made me feel that I was loved. The day before Barbara left for Maine we talked and she asked, how was the book coming? I told her I was a little busy and had not got to it for a while. She said, "Don't you think you should get it out?" Those were her last words to me. So this book has a special dedication to you Barbara, where you will always remain in my heart.

Acknowledgements

To my editor, Lisa Graziano (Author of "*Hell's Creek*")

Thank you so very much for your endless help and inspiration. You not only edited my book but went the distance with me and believed in my subject matter and how it could impact both young and old.

Lisa, I have witnessed the interactions between you and your daughter, and the love in both your eyes shines like a beacon, and you always show so much love for her. Lisa, you are a wonderful mother and I see how well you communicate with your 'little one'. Most assuredly she will grow up to become a caring and loving young woman like yourself.

Thank you again, you will always be an important part of my life.

Cover designer Joe Carty

Hoping you know how much I appreciated you taking the time from your own busy schedule, and helping me to choose this suitable cover that wraps around this phenomenon we call, self abuse.

My sincerest gratitude and thanks to all the prophesiers and wonderful staff at *The Cape Cod Community College*. After reading my book, *Look Beyond The Scars*, you will have a better understanding of why it was so hard for me to be in college. At times, when I wasn't able to comprehend the course load, you never gave up on me. You guided me in the right direction when I needed it most. You gave me your time even though I am a little older than some of you. I thank God for my teachers, for without you, I would have never have experienced how wonderful learning can be and what it means to have an education. I value each one of you. You were my savior and I thank you from the very bottom of my heart.

"Look Beyond the Scars" is a moving account of a personal journey out of a painful existence into a rewarding and fulfilling life. Connie's story alludes to the lack of knowledge of self-harm and the absence of a treatment modalities in the past while also revealing the magnitude of the work still to be done. This book will enlighten those not only in the mental health field working with adults and children, but also those in education, community and family life by providing them with insight into identifying behaviors associated with self-mutilation."

"Dialectical Behavioral Therapy (DBT) has made immeasurable progress in the treatment of self-harm. DBT combines Cognitive Behavioral Therapy (CBT) with Mindfulness through the teaching of skills with the goal of acceptance and implementing change resulting in renowned success in the treatment of self-harm."

—Lorraine A. Touchette,
MSW, LISCW
DBT Skills Center
West Yarmouth, Massachusetts

Chapter One

I walked behind the tall dark-haired nurse, listening to the clanging of her heavy keys hitting the chain that drooped from the front of her dress to her pocket, the noise echoing in my ears as I followed behind her down the long empty, darkened hallway. I knew that each step was bringing us closer to the room at the end where I knew I would suffer more pain than I was already in. It was late. All the patients were in bed. The lights were out except for the night-lights dimly shining on the floor at the end of each four-bed dorm we passed. My hands throbbed from the sutures needed to repair the damage I had done by breaking several windows. Every now and then, the nurse would turn and shine her flashlight in my eyes, then slowly drop the light to the bloody bandages on both my hands.

When we finally reached the seclusion room, she unlocked the door and the heat hit my face. It was always devastatingly hot in there. She gestured me in with a wave of her flashlight. The night-light in the room was much brighter than the ones in the hallway and I could see, in the middle of the room on the floor, the hard black rubber mattress that I would push with my feet to the corner of the room the minute she left and locked the door. I would curl up in the corner, like a kitten, so they would have a hard time seeing me through the five-by-seven-inch window in the door.

Boston State Hospital

Each time they made their rounds (which was not too often), they tried peering in the little window and finally had to open the door to check on me. That was when I welcomed the little breeze that came from the hallway. Again, the flashlight searched my face and then my hands. This time she held two rolls of bandages. She never opened her mouth, nor did I, except to ask for a glass of water. As she knelt down beside me on the mattress, she wrapped each hand, going over the bloody bandages that were already in place. I just kept my head down. When she left, I could feel the tears wanting to come, but I just could not let go. I sipped on the glass of warm water, slowly falling off to sleep as my mind became deadened to the pain that was flowing through my hands, my mind, my heart, and my soul.

Now when I think of my youth and how I lost it to not one but many of these state hospitals in Massachusetts, I can see that the doctors and hospital staff just did not know what to do with fifteen-year-old girls who were cutting themselves.

My name is Connie. I was born the youngest of five children. My father was a chef, and my mother was a homemaker.

Myself, 1945

I am a survivor of my own holocaust, my youth lost to self-mutilation. I was a "cutter." My form of self-injury involved cutting myself with razor blades and broken glass. My physical scars are hidden under clothing. The psychological scars have been buried deep within until now, in my midlife, when I feel the need to explore and share what caused me to do such things to myself. My hope is that my revelations will help anyone who feels now as I did then and help them know that they are not alone and that there can be a brighter future. I write this book, based on my life, in the hope of reaching a new generation of self-injurers.

Chapter Two

The *Boston Globe* reported in a December 2003 article, "There are an estimated three million people nationwide who engage in moderate or superficial self-mutilation." The article went on to quote Barry Walsh, executive director of the Bridge of Central Massachusetts: "Once considered as a symptom of other psychological illnesses, it is now viewed by many health professionals as its own severe and potentially progressive phenomenon."

The research on this subject provides many different professional opinions on the forms, reasons, and treatment for self-injury. Self-injury can consist of cutting (with razors, glass, knives, pins, or any other sharp object), burning, head banging, hair pulling, and severe nail biting (biting and tearing at the nails until they bleed); It is the act of inflicting physical harm which, in turn, causes damage to bodily tissue

There are many reasons people choose to harm themselves in this way, including physical or emotional neglect and physical or sexual abuse. Feeling enraged by what goes on around them, some people turn to self-abuse to somehow get control of what they feel is an otherwise out-of-control situation. Many say that the self-injury is followed by a "controlled calm."

Today, there are many programs available to help those who self-injure. *We are in dire need of more programs with a safe environment.*

Back in my day, the health profession didn't have any idea why we were doing this and had not a clue on how to treat us. This then is my story.

The first time I hurt myself was during school. I scratched my arm with a staple and then told my teacher I accidentally scratched it on a screw so that she would send me to the nurse's office and I could get out of class. The scratching escalated into cutting deeper with razor blades and glass. I would drink, cut myself deeply, and go home. I always cleaned up and bandaged my cuts so my mother would not see this, and I always wore long sleeves. Sometimes my mother would ask me what happened to my arms, and I would lie. I do believe in my heart that she knew what I was doing but just did not know what to say to me.

At the age of seven, a male neighbor molested me. I didn't even know what sex was, but something told me that what he was doing was very wrong, and I was afraid to tell anyone. Maybe it was the way I was brought up; I came from a very strict Irish Catholic family where love and affection were not easily shown. We never discussed sex in our home. As I look back now, I know we should have.

It happened again, several times, when I was thirteen. I never opened my mouth. I just buried it because I felt ashamed and dirty. I don't want to sound like some of those talk shows on TV, so I'm not going to go into a lot of sad details. All I can say is that I felt dirty, guilty, and so ashamed, always thinking it was my fault.

I missed a great deal of school due to ear infections and a serious infection in my arm (from a cat scratch), which required an operation and seemed to take forever to heal. It was later discovered that I had a hole in my eardrum. And I was a very slow learner. How could they expect me to catch up? It seemed that every paper I got back was wrong, so I believe I just gave up. In grammar school, I was put into the first of three special classes.

The teacher was so overweight that she was tired all the time. All she would do was have us color. I was a great drawer, so she would have me draw on the blackboard all the time. Every day, she had a new theme for me to draw. She would read from a book, and we would have to follow along with her.

She always had a can of soup for lunch. The big deal was for everyone in the class to raise their hands, and she would pick one of us to go to her closet at the back of the room and get her hot plate and can of soup. For some reason, she made us feel that we were doing something special for her when, all the time, it was because she had so much trouble moving around because of her weight. She made us feel special being chosen to wash the blackboard, empty the pencil sharpener, straighten up the books on her desk, and clap the erasers. Clapping the erasers was my favorite because it meant going outside, and I would take my sweet time doing it. When I was through, there was not one speck of chalk left in those erasers.

I remember so vividly what would happen if we misbehaved in class. This teacher had a piece of wood, which was actually a three-sided piece of molding, and we had to put our hands out in front of her, and she would whack us three times. God forbid if anybody should cry. I remember it hurting terribly, and I had welts across my fingers for the whole day. It seemed that every teacher used this method of discipline. It was called "the rat hand." If I told my mother when I got home, she would say, "That's what you get for doing wrong." I was always doing something wrong. I would be hit even if I was just talking in class. It's a wonder they didn't beat me to death.

Every day when lunch was over, the teacher would fall asleep reading to us. Every now and then, she would pick her head up and ask one of us to come and stand beside her and read aloud to the class. One day, she asked me to come up. I was struggling through my part of the book when I saw her head and chin resting on her big bosom. I started to make up words, and then I began throwing in some swear words. I was the class clown because I was ashamed of how dumb I really felt. Each time she told me to read, I did this. The other kids laughed as I said the swear words, and then the teacher would pick her head up ever so slowly and say, "Very good, Constance, now take your seat." Then she would call the next kid. That was the extent of my day in her room.

School was a nightmare for other girls too. It was great for some kids, but I had such a hard time fitting in. I was so tall and skinny, with straggly hair and bad teeth. My older sister, Mary, tried to help me fit in somewhere; but I always felt out of place.

I remember being in school, and my mind would start to wander. I would just stare out of the window, and I couldn't wait to get the hell out of there. From grade school, I went on to junior high assigned to another "special" class. One would think that in a class that was special I would get the help I needed. Not so! Special classes in those days were set up for "dummies." My classroom was in the basement with the boys' woodworking shop on one side and the bathrooms on the other. We also had a separate entrance from the rest of the school. They made us use the back door, the door that was used for fire drills. That only furthered our sense of isolation. The boys would file past our classroom to get to the woodworking shop, and some would stop and put their fingers up to their heads in a circular motion while mouthing the word "dummy." What a rotten feeling that was!

My first project with wood in 1970s.

I loved the smell of the woodworking shop. Of course, back in those days, girls were not allowed to attend that class. Boy, would I have loved to be in woodworking. I was very good with my hands, and I believe even then I had an innate ability to create from wood. I had learned from my dad. But no one cared or even noticed my interest. We did not have counselors back then. If we had, maybe they would have seen my potential, and I might have been a great architect today. Had I been allowed to participate, maybe I would have indulged in creativity instead of cutting.

Another project I built myself

If I did something wrong in class (which was quite frequently), my teacher would make me stand out in the hallway. Little did she know I loved it. I loved looking through the glass window of the door where the boys were working. They were making birdhouses, shoeshine boxes, and tie racks. Sometimes the boys would catch me looking in and tell their teacher. The fools thought I was interested in them. Boy, would I have loved to have been doing woodworking.

Well, time just kept passing. The longer I was in that class, the dumber I felt; and with all those feelings bottled up inside of me, things only got worse. My teacher did not like me very much. I don't know if it was a personality conflict or because I could never grasp what she was trying to teach. I believe she was very frustrated with her job, trying to teach kids who were "unteachable." I also believe she was close to retirement although she looked well over eighty at the time. She had white hair and wore those heavy black shoes with the laces untied most of the time. She was a little eccentric. Now, when I think back, I see how hard it must have been for her, being stuck in that basement with kids who just would not or could not learn. She must have gone home each day with the smell of the bathrooms and the sawdust in her nose, hating it.

Do you know what it feels like when you don't fit in, when you are face-to-face with one of your peers and no one is around to hear the cruel things they are saying to you? You watch them walk away with their hundred-dollar sneakers, Tommy shirts, and cologne; and they are laughing at you while you are left standing there in your secondhand clothes feeling like shit. This can all add up in a kid's head and make her feel so rotten inside that she feels she has nothing left to lose. Even her own life means nothing.

I believe that this would be helped somewhat by having a dress code. This is something that could have been done even back in the fifties when I was in school wearing my sisters' hand-me-downs and clothes from the secondhand store. I remember that feeling when some kid would comment on my old clothes.

Some days, a bus would come to the school to take us to Forsythe Dental School (a part of Tufts University). It was the bus from hell, not only for me but for many of the other kids who feared the dentist as well. I hated to go because they hurt me so much the very first time I went.

When we arrived, we were told to follow the colored line on the floor, and that would lead us to the room where the dentist would see us. Not me! I would go just so far along that line and then hide under the stairwell. They would never miss me because there were so many of us, including kids from other schools. It's awful to think that the experience has left me with such a frightful feeling about dentists. To this day, when I do go to the dentist, my hands sweat and my heart pounds so loud I can hardly hear anyone speaking to me. I feel so much stress. I have to relate this to any dentist I see now so that they would understand how terrified I am and will take it slow and try to make me more comfortable and pain free.

I had to take cooking and sewing in school. I liked cooking because that is what my father did for a living. I did not like sewing though. One day in sewing class I took some common pins and stuck them in the soft part of my skin. It didn't hurt, and I wasn't trying to hurt myself; I was just trying to be funny. I made a circle of pins around the palm of my hand. I called to one of the girls in my class, and when she caught sight of my hand waving in the air, she let out one loud screech. That was it; the teacher caught me, and I had to go stand out in the hallway. I remember the principal walking by me with his head bowed low. I could hear some of his muttering: "Oh, you again. You will never learn." He never looked up at me, and I could not make out what else he was saying, but I knew it wasn't pleasant.

Reflecting back on my cooking teacher, I recall the feeling I would get when it came time to leave the basement and climb the stairs to her room. I loved cooking. I am not sure if it was because my dad was a chef or because of the freedom I felt every time I got out of that so-called classroom in the basement. But it is one of the few nice things to look back on.

My cooking teacher was young and easy to talk to, and I often asked her to keep me after class to help clean the pantry. She would let me stay even if she didn't need help because she knew how much I hated to go back downstairs to that miserable classroom. I'd go into the pantry and mess around, taking the paraffin and a little knife to carve animals. It was quite a mess, but I always made sure to clean up real well before I left.

Sometimes I just sat and talked with her at her desk while she was doing her paperwork. I always asked a lot of questions—do you have a boyfriend, where do you live, when are you going to get married? She had long blonde hair and wore the most wonderful-smelling perfume. She always talked to me like I was a real person, not the stupid kid that I felt I was.

I loved to see her waiting for the bus. As soon as school was out, I would make a beeline for the bus stop; we had to go to the same station, and that gave me more time to spend with her. I never talked too much about myself. I always directed the conversations back to her. God forbid she should find out about me and the abuse; I would have been devastated. That was the last thing I would have told her or anyone else back then. When we got to our stop, she would catch a train, and I would have to get another bus. I remember always looking to see if her train was in the station and hoping that it wasn't there or that if it was, it would pull out before she got off the bus. Then we would have more time to talk together. Oh, how lonely a child I was. There was so much pain inside.

I had her class once a week, and her room was right across from the nursing office. Sometimes I scratched my arm (in the "special" class) so the teacher would send me to the nurse. If my cooking teacher was in between classes, I'd knock on her door, and she would wave me into the classroom. I'd immediately ask if she needed the pantry cleaned so that I'd have a good reason to stay. She would say no but ask why I was not in my classroom. I told her that I had an accident and scratched my arm and was going to see the nurse. She would stay with me in the nurses' office until I was bandaged up and then send me back to my room. I don't believe she was aware of just how bad that so-called classroom really was.

Then I had the long walk back downstairs to the dungeon. Once, I went in the woodworking shop when no one was around. I felt like a kid in a candy shop, touching all the tools and looking up close at what the boys were working on. I remember thinking, *Oh, how I wish I was coming to this class instead of next door.*

All of a sudden, I heard a loud voice yelling at me, "What are you doing in here? Get back to your classroom right now! This room is for boys only!" Again, I had that horrible feeling of having done something wrong. Girls were forbidden in that room, but I didn't care; I went there every chance I got.

Well, I walked back into my dungeon classroom; and my teacher didn't even remember where I had gone or why, never mind that my arm was scratched and had a bandage on it. She looked at me and said, "Constance, take your seat and open your book to this page." How I hated that name, especially when she would say it. She was reading from the book, as usual, and the class was following along like little puppies. I just could not help myself; I would end up staring out the window and daydreaming. I hated where I was and who I was. I truly believe that if I was in a regular classroom, it might have made a world of difference.

No teachers ever came downstairs to see our room; they had no reason to go there. And if our teacher ever left the room, she always put one of the older and nicer girls in charge. She would never ask me—she knew I would have opened the doors and let everyone go home!

I just could not deal with all those feelings. My main point is what took place after the fact. After all the abuse I suffered in school—not only from the kids but also from the teachers—and the abuse that went on in the neighborhood, the self-abuse took over my life. It started with little scratches and escalated to razor blades and broken glass. I could not control it; it was something I had to do, no matter what.

After school, I could at least look forward to softball practice with my church. Two nights a week, we played. I played with all my heart. They had junior and senior teams, and because my sister Mary didn't care for softball, I signed up for the senior team in her name. I was so tall that I was able to pass for a senior, and this way, I could play for both teams. The teams had their games at different fields, so no one was aware of what I was doing.

Then one Saturday, all hell broke loose. The junior team forfeited their game and decided to come and watch the seniors play. I had no place to hide. There I was playing left field when I looked over and saw the two coaches talking together. When the inning was over, both of them were waving me in. It was the longest walk of my life. I had lied, and now I was caught; there was no way of getting around this. As I reached the coaches, they asked me, "Are you Connie or Mary, and how old are you?" I apologized but told them that I just really wanted to play as much softball as I could. They informed me that from that moment on, I was on the junior team. I was just surprised that they let me continue to play at all! They knew I was good, could play any position, and really loved the game; so they allowed me to stay.

Chapter Three

Back in my neighborhood, they had what we called the Denison House. It was a place where children could go to play and make friends. It was on Howard Avenue, Durchester Massachusetts. Well, anyway, it was something like the boys' clubs they have today; but girls were welcome also. It had a great big gym and ping-pong tables. There was a hall where sock hop dances were held, but of course, I stayed in the other room and played ping-pong. I was always embarrassed about my looks, and I knew none of the boys were going to ask me to dance. I didn't mind, or at least I didn't think I did. Today, you can't drag me off the dance floor—I get lost in the music.

The Denison House 1950s

Every Monday night, they held cooking classes upstairs at the Denison House. It was great fun. Then the cooking classes stopped; they were looking for a new teacher for one night a week. I asked my father if he would come up on his night off and teach the class. He said, "Sure!" As a chef, he was a great teacher, and I loved having him there. I felt so proud of him, but to this day, I don't know if he got paid or if he had volunteered. When they finally got a full-time teacher, my dad didn't need to come anymore. It was just as good because I remember being very jealous when he gave the other girls more attention. I guess that was because I never saw that much of him when we were home. I'd come home from school just as he'd be going to work. He worked nights and slept most of the day. I missed those Monday night cooking classes with him and the time we spent together.

The Denison House also sent children to camp in the summer. The name of the camp was, of course, Camp Denison. I came from the city, so being in the country was a treat.

When we first arrived at camp, we were all given empty mattress covers, and we had to fill them with straw. My mattress was so big it looked like a three-in-one! After a couple of nights sleeping on it, it finally flattened out. Once I learned to swim, the instructors couldn't get me out of the water. When I finally came out, they said I looked like a prune.

It was great waking up in the morning and seeing all the trees around me; I loved the smell of pine. When I wrote to my family, I put some pine needles in the envelope, hoping my mom and sisters would smell them and love it as much as I did.

We were up very early every morning to make up our bunk beds, wash up, and race to the mess hall. Outside the mess hall was a huge flagpole where we all gathered and say the Pledge of Allegiance. I thought that was so cool. Then we all filed into the mess hall where breakfast was waiting for us; boy, did I love the smell of that place. They had everything you could imagine. My favorites were the biscuits. They were as big as your plate. Well, maybe not quite that big, but they sure looked it when I was little.

We all sat at a long wooden table, four of us on each side and a counselor at the head. The counselor would stand and say a prayer and then direct our attention to the teepee on the mantle over the fireplace. We all knew that whichever table was the quietest and cleanest would get the teepee and keep it on the table until someone else won. Well, I could never stop talking, so I don't remember our table ever winning.

There was also a pet raccoon that wandered around the mess hall. I loved this little guy, and he would come and sit on my lap and let me pet him. To this day, I love all living creatures. Now I have a friend squirrel; she sits in my lap and eats peanuts and sometimes plays with my cat.

One girl at the camp really bothered me. She was overweight and stepped on a toad and killed it. I was so upset that I yelled at her and called her names. She was telling everyone that she didn't mean to do it, but she was obviously lying. I hated her for doing that. Of course, now I think back and have a different perspective. I believe now that she must have been very lonely because everyone made fun of her weight and she didn't have any friends there. It was her way of getting some much-needed attention.

One afternoon, it had started to rain quite hard; and the camp counselors ran around in their army green rain gear, trying to gather everyone up like sheepdogs with a flock. When the counselors were out of sight, I ran back outside and started to play around. I loved playing in the rain and had done so at home so often that I thought nothing of it. Well, it was a hurricane, not a rainstorm. I remember running around, and it started to get really windy, and the branches from the trees were falling down all around me. When I saw the counselor coming after me, I decided to play hide-and-seek. She didn't appreciate that very much; and when she caught up to me, she grabbed me by the arm, swung me around, and yelled, "Are you crazy? Running around like this in such a bad storm, you could catch a cold and be sick for the rest of the week! Look at your clothes! They're soaked through." She must have thought I was such a brat.

When we finally got back to the recreation hall, she wrapped me up in a warm blanket and had me lie down on the floor next to the fireplace. It felt good, so warm and cozy. She pulled up a chair and sat beside me. Every now and then, her hand dropped down and landed ever so softly on my back, and she would rub my back to see if my shirt was drying. For that brief moment, I felt safe. Thank you, Ellie, wherever you are!

There was always something going on at the camp. I remember one time we camped out overnight up on a hill with a big tower nearby. Early the next morning, a few of the girls and I stared to run around and play tag. I decided to run under the tower, but I was so tall that I ran smack into the iron slat head-on. I had a bump in the middle of my head the size of a baseball. The sound when I hit was so loud that the counselor came running over and took me to the lake to put cold water on my head. I think she was afraid that I had really hurt myself, but I felt fine and couldn't wait to get back to playing tag.

Chapter Four

Let's go back as far as I can remember. Some little vague memory sticks in my head. You have to know I came from an old Irish Catholic family where we were taught to hold everything in and not speak until spoken to. In this memory, I can see my mother lying down on her bed crying and my father putting his finger up to his lips, telling me to be quiet. As he was shutting the bedroom door behind him, I felt her pain. I felt sad and did not know why. That is all I remember. I was very young, and my mother was dealing with the loss of my four-month-old brother.

Back then, I guess that was the way women dealt with the loss of a child—shove it down and do not talk about it. I cannot tell you how long this went on, but I believe that it is something one never gets over, and my mother was no exception. Being hushed and left out of what was going on was a typical coping mechanism in my family. Maybe that is why I was seeking love and affection elsewhere.

I was always a tomboy; I could do anything the boys could, even better. I recall later in life a neighbor telling my mom that she used to watch me ride my bike down the hill; I would stand up on the seat, holding on to the handlebars. When I roller-skated, she said it looked like I had taken lessons. I was very good at such things because I loved what I was doing, and when you love something that much, you put your heart and soul into it. I was always told that young ladies didn't do things like that.

When I was seven or eight years old, my girlfriend Crystal and I liked to sit in the hallway of her house. Back then, everyone on the street lived in a three-family house; it was an Irish and Italian neighborhood. It was hard for me because I was so tall, and Crystal was so short. Everywhere we went together, people would pat her on the head and ask if she was my little sister and comment on how cute she was. But we were the same age. Funny how things can bother us without us knowing why, but I still loved Crystal like a sister. She was someone I could share my fantasies with and know that she understood and felt the same way I did.

Crystal and I often got together just to sit and talk about a certain television show that was on at that time (*Decoy* with Beverly Garland). We both wished that Beverly Garland was our mother. We were crazy about her. Crystal must have felt the same way I did because we could not wait to be alone and fantasize about having other people for our mothers. Out of all of them, Beverly Garland was our favorite.

We would talk about some of the women we knew and how we wished one of them could be our mother. I do believe we just needed someone to show us that we were lovable. There are children born into families that don't give enough physical contact. Those children need to be held more and reassured all the time that they are loved. If you do not have that as a child, I believe you go searching for it and try to get it any way you can. In my case, I felt ashamed and dirty because of the men who had put their hands on me. I was looking for a mother who could hold me and tell me that she loved me, that the abuse was not my fault, and that everything would be okay.

Poor Crystal lost a sister, and they waked her in the living room of their house. I remember walking into the living room and seeing her in the casket. She was in a long white dress and had beautiful blonde hair. To me, she looked like she was asleep. I was too young to realize what was really going on. I did not even know what death was. I just know I felt strange and scared. I did not go all the way up to the casket. I turned around and left.

Crystal's mother has drinking problems, and it seemed she was always drinking. Her father was hardly ever home due to his work. My mother never drank, but the loss of my little brother put her into some kind of a depression. I guess she just could not reach out to me, and I needed her so desperately. I needed to be held, and I needed to feel wanted. I know now that those were the things I was missing. My mother loved me without words.

Today, in my heart, I understand what she must have been going through. I know it was no fault of hers. She did the best she could, and as a mother myself, I do the best I can.

It's kind of sad when I think about back then—there were no support groups like there are now, so those poor mothers just had to hold it all inside. The loss of a child has to be the worst feeling in the world. How could anyone be expected to carry on as though nothing had happened?

Chapter Five

My sister Jane was engaged to be married. My father was a heavy drinker at the time. I do not have any memories of his drinking, but my sisters do. He was a quiet drinker. Well, as time grew closer to the wedding, he quit drinking; and we moved. I was fourteen years old. We moved to another three-family house about a block away. In this house, I had my own room. Before that, I had been in a room with my two sisters and, before that, with Mom and Dad on a little sofa. Jane got married and started a family right away, a family of eight children. I spent a lot of time at Jane's house.

When I was fifteen, I was introduced to alcohol. I used to go to a place called the Spa, something like Arnold's from *Happy Days*. In fact, it was just like Arnold's. It was very popular back in the fifties and sixties, giving teenagers a place to go and sit with a Coke and hamburger. The jukebox was always playing in the background. My favorite song was "Love Me Tender." How I wished someone could have loved me tender.

That was where I met some new friends. They'd get the older boys to buy beer, and that was when I started to drink. I was not as popular as the rest of the girls, but I didn't care. I just tagged along as long as I could drink. The girls liked me somewhat, but the boys would not give me a second look. I was very tall and skinny, and my teeth were in rough shape, so I tried to keep my mouth shut when I was around the boys.

My drinking started with beer, and then it progressed to whiskey. We would find an empty field or hallway where we would drink, and then we would go back to the Spa. One night, it was snowing so hard we could barely walk, but I had a few drinks in me, so I didn't care. After we got back to the Spa, I wanted more to drink. I begged one of the guys to get me a half-pint of whiskey, and finally, he did. I waited outside around the corner so no one could see him give me the bottle. I thanked him and headed for an abandoned house where I could drink.

The snow was getting deeper. I was so very cold as I finally reached the empty house. I was all by myself, and I didn't care. I went inside and sat in a corner of the cellar where we had some crates set up. I started to drink the whiskey, and at first, I felt good. But as I drank more, I started to cry. I don't know why. Finally, I finished the bottle and headed down to the Spa. It was still snowing heavily. I remember falling every now and then, but I would get up and keep walking. For some reason, I was laughing and crying at the same time. I never felt the cold. When I finally got to the Spa, it was closed. All the lights were off except for a dim light coming from the jukebox. I remember feeling very lonely realizing that everyone had gone home. It was so pretty. All the streetlights were on, and the snow was so white. I just wanted to keep walking. I had mixed emotions at the time. I wanted to cut myself, but I was too cold and too drunk to think much about it.

I didn't want to go home, so I kept walking until I got to my friend's house. I rang the doorbell, and she came down. I told her that my mother would kill me if she saw me this way. She said that if her mother saw me, she would make me go home, so she let me stay in her cellar. Beside the furnace, it was nice and warm. I finally fell asleep; and the next day when I went home, my mother asked me where I had been, and I told her I stayed at my friend's house because it had snowed so heavily.

That was when drinking became a big part of my life. All the girls drank. One other girl cut herself also but not badly. That was the start of my cutting. After we drank, we would cut ourselves, and then she would leave and go back to the Spa. But I'd stay and drink some more and then cut myself more deeply. I would go home and—before my mother could see what I had done—go into the bathroom, clean up, and put a bandage on. I always wore long sleeves so that no one could tell what I was doing. Then I would go into my bedroom, lie on the bed, and listen to music. I would finally fall asleep. Sometimes, the next day, my mother would ask me what happened to my arm; I would lie and tell her some tall story.

I did have some good times and some good friends at the Spa. Most of them did not know what I was going through or doing to myself, and the ones that did just accepted me as I was. Some days, I was fine; and others, I just did not know when I was going to pick up a razor and start hacking at myself. I remember the empty feeling in the pit of my stomach; I was feeling lonely even when I was with friends. I would tell them I was going home, but I would go off and abuse myself.

The best memories I have of the Spa are from the time when my sister Mary worked there as a soda jerk. She was great, and the owners loved her. She was so good with the customers. Every time I went in and ordered something, no matter what it was, Mary always gave me extras. She always was so kind to me.

It was a ritual; every night after supper, we headed for the Spa. Back in those days, children would go out early and come home early. Sometimes my friend Dottie would come to the house to call for me, and she would have to wait in the living room. In my house, we had to kneel down after supper and say the rosary. My mother always seemed to time the meal just right so that when we finished supper, it was time to say the rosary along with Cardinal Cushing on the radio. Mary and I would try to eat slowly, but it didn't matter; my mother still made sure we said the rosary.

I remember one night, we were having mashed potatoes, and Mom got up from the table to get something from the fridge. Mary put a big spoon of potatoes in her mouth and started to squeeze them through her teeth. It looked just like worms. All of a sudden, Mom caught sight of Mary out of the corner of her eye and slapped her on the back of the head. The potatoes went flying all over the place. I don't believe Mom knew just how much Mary had in her mouth. We all cracked up with laughter, but not Mom; she had one thing on her mind, and that was the rosary. I often wonder if Mom laughed inwardly or even when we left the house to go out that evening. I sure hope so because to this day, we still laugh about it ourselves.

My sister Mary would kneel down at her chair, with me on the other side kneeling at my chair, and Mom at the head of the table. Every now and then, I would pick up the tablecloth, and Mary was doing the same. I'd make some kind of funny face, trying to make Mary laugh, and she would be making faces back at me. We always tried to do something to make the time go by faster.

Beside the Spa, we would go to a little restaurant that was run by a Polish family. Crystal and I liked to talk to the daughter of the owner. She was much older than we were. The mother and two daughters ran the place, and they were all hard workers. Crystal and I thought how nice it would be to have someone like her for a mother. How sad to think back and want another mother so badly. What was it that Crystal and I wanted from this woman? I felt that if she knew me and what had happened to me, she would hate me. God knows I hated myself enough. I felt it was my fault because I let those men touch me. According to my Catholic upbringing, I was going to burn in hell for what had happened to me. I felt I was bad; I was my own judge and jury.

Chapter Six

At the age of fifteen and a half, I pleaded with my dad to please sign the form so I could quit school; I told him I would get a job immediately. When he finally signed the papers, it set me free. I can't tell you how much I hated school!

I worked a couple of factory jobs, which to me felt more like being in prison than school had. I was required to stay in one spot too long; and of course, being Miss Fidgety, I was always trying to walk around. When they finally let me go, it felt like a pardon from prison.

Ever since I was a young girl, I had wanted to be a nurse, but in my heart, I knew that this was never going to happen for me because I had been labeled as "dumb." I knew that the next best thing to being a nurse would be a nurse's aid. So I went to every nursing home and hospital I could find. They all said the same thing: "You don't have any experience."

Then one day, my mom told me that she had read something in the church bulletin about the nuns teaching a home-nursing course. She suggested that we both sign up, so we did. I believe the course lasted about four weeks, two nights each week. It was great not only because I was getting a chance to learn something I so desperately wanted to learn, but because my mom was doing it with me. When we finished the course, the nuns gave us a slip of paper showing that we had graduated and a little pin that read Home Nursing. To this day, I still have that pin.

I still was not a nurse's aid, but I did learn a great deal that could help me get a decent job helping people. I often wonder why my mother took that course with me. I think she might have been trying, in her own way, to give me more confidence. She knew how much I wanted to work as a nurse's aid.

Later in life, I found out that my own mother had to leave school at a very young age. There were ten in her family, and she was the oldest. She left the country of Ireland ("the old country" as she called it) and came to America to work in a factory and send the money back home to help her family. I can imagine that over the years, she must have kept a great deal bottled up inside. We were not the type of family that talked, hugged, or kissed. Somehow we were supposed to know that we were loved. I was the youngest of five children with two brothers and two sisters. My oldest sister says that I was the one who needed the hugs and kisses more than the rest of them. I believe that was true; but I feel that every child needs to feel comforted, loved, and made to feel secure.

One of the first jobs I had after the factory was as an usherette in downtown Boston. The area was very upscale back in the fifties. I wore a little red uniform and had to carry a flashlight to show people to their seats. I remember that when it wasn't too crowded, I would give people better seats than the ones they'd bought the tickets for, if there were empty seats. I figured it would be all right. After a while, people started to give me tips for finding them better seats. I did not expect tips. I just wanted to be kind to people so they would like me. One night, up in the mezzanine, I had moved people around; and someone was unhappy about not having the seat he had paid for. The manager was called, and the lights were turned on. To his surprise, everyone was in the wrong seat. I didn't get fired although I still don't know why.

One of the really cool things about working in the theater was that I got to see my first musical, *South Pacific*. I was fascinated! I watched it many times and absolutely loved Mary Martin's character, Nelly Forbush. I learned all the dialogue and songs from the show, and one sticks in my head to this day: "You've Got to Be Carefully Taught." We all need to remember those words and learn from them:

> You've got to be taught
> To hate and fear.
> And to hate all the people your relatives hate.
> To be afraid of people whose eyes are oddly made,
> And people whose skin is a different shade.

I came home one day after an interview for yet another nursing home and, again, had no luck. It was my dad's day off, and he was sitting at the kitchen table having a cup of tea. He asked how I had done. I told him I was tired of being turned down, and I started to cry, something I never liked to do. It was all starting to feel so hopeless. In his very soft voice, he told me to get a cup of tea and sit down and join him; he wanted to talk to me. These are the words he planted in my head that long-ago day in the kitchen: "Connie, the next time you go on an interview and they say you don't have enough experience or there are no openings, I want you to ask if they can possibly use you anywhere. Laundry, kitchen, mopping floors, whatever. Just get your foot in the door!" That moment will stay in my head forever.

The next interview was at the Joseph P. Kennedy Hospital for handicapped children in Brighton, Massachusetts. Again, I heard those words "I am very sorry, but there are no openings right now."

I remembered what my father had said, and I went for it, the words just falling out of my mouth. "I'll do anything!" The nun got up and said she would be right back. She was not gone long; and when she came back in, she asked if I wanted to work in the laundry room and clean up around the wards. Well, you would have thought she'd given me a million dollars. I immediately asked, "When can I start?"

She said that the next morning would be just fine and shook my hand, saying, "I'll see you in the morning."

I couldn't wait to get home and tell my dad the good news. Bless his heart and kind manner. They had landed me a job exactly where I wanted to be.

My Dad

Some nights as I lie in my room wide awake,
I listen for his car; I can tell by his brakes.
I listen to his footsteps as he goes through the hall,
Telling myself, he is the biggest man of all.
I lay there so still, not moving a limb,
Wishing I could jump up and throw my arms around him.

Sometimes I get up, and into the kitchen I go,
He turns with a smile, and then says a hello.
He sits down at the table, and I make him some tea,
Then he takes off his shoes and reads the paper to me.

Mother always makes two sandwiches for him
leaves them in the refrigerator, with a note for Big Jim.
He works every night and sleeps through the day,
I don't see much of him; it seems goodbye is all we say.

Mother is always right there to call him at three,
They sit and discuss things over a cup of tea.
Then he is up in a flash and in to shave
I walk by the door, and I get just a wave.

It seems like a very unhappy and lonely life,
But the real one I feel bad for is my mother, his wife.

My dad was such a kind and gentle soft-spoken man. He never had a bad word to say about anyone. Oh, how I wish I could have talked to him and told him what had happened to me when I was so young. But I was afraid he would hate me.

One day, when I was cleaning up the kitchen at the Kennedy Hospital, a supervisor came in and said she wanted to see me in her office when I was finished. She said she had something she wanted to discuss with me. I thought they were going to let me go. Well, to my surprise, it was just the opposite. She said there was a position open for a nurse's aid and asked if I would like the job. No hesitation on my part! I jumped at the chance. My dad's advice had really worked. I got my foot in the door, and now I was finally going to be a nurse's aid.

Thank you, Dad, for having faith in me. Over the years, your words have guided me more than once. I love you and will always miss you.

With the new position came a great deal of responsibility. I learned how to get the patients cleaned up, put braces on those who needed to go for physical therapy, and help those who were going for counseling. Every afternoon, weather permitting, the patients went out into the big yard where there was always something going on. I remember one little boy in a wheelchair who was a bit of a loner. I made it a point of going over to him and asking if he wanted me to draw pictures in the dirt for him. He loved the game we played; I would draw an animal, and he would try to guess what it was. Sometimes I drew something with two heads, and he would laugh so hard that his whole chair shook. I loved to make him laugh.

The cardinal dropped by the play area to say hello to all the kids. He came over to the little boy and asked him what was so funny. The child pointed to the two-headed bird I had drawn in the dirt. The cardinal let out a laugh. Then he put his hand on my shoulder and said, "Young lady, you are doing a great job. Keep it up." I felt so good for a moment, and then I started to think of my past. Yes, it did feel good; but somewhere in the pit of my stomach, I felt like shit and didn't feel I deserved his kind words. That's the way it was with me for a very long time. The more people complimented me, the worse I felt about myself and my dirty little secrets.

I went from job to job after the Kennedy Hospital. I spent a great deal of time in nursing homes. Every one of my supervisors begged me to go back to school to get my high school diploma. I was very good with the patients, and the nurses would let me do things that the aids were not supposed to do. I just kept telling them that I would go back to school someday. I knew in my own mind that I was never going back. It was not because I didn't want to; it was that I felt so dumb. When we are young, we don't see what others see as special in ourselves. I was also terribly afraid that someone was going to find out my big secret—not just being in a special class, but also about my self-abuse. Not until we get older do we start to think about what we are really made of and who we are and why we did the things we did.

Chapter Seven

One evening, Crystal and I went into the Polish family's restaurant. They had a jukebox, and I went behind it and turned it up because they kept it so low we could hardly hear it. The daughter came over, turned it back down, and told me not to turn it up again or I would have to leave. I did turn it up again, and she told me to get out and not come back. I had to leave, but Crystal could stay. I went outside, leaned against the window, and watched Crystal and the daughter talking. I banged on the window every now and then to get their attention. Crystal was sitting up at the end of the counter where the two sisters would stand all the time and have coffee until the customers came in. I banged on the window again until Crystal came out. I asked her to go back in, tell the family that I was sorry, and ask if I could come back. I felt so bad. She went in and spoke to them, but they said I could not come in. I got mad and told Crystal that since she was my friend, she should come out with me, and she agreed.

We both started banging on the window of the restaurant until one of the sisters came out and chased us away. Now Crystal was told not to come back either. That made us angry, so we kept it up. We would open the door and yell inside just to get them mad enough to chase us again. We kept this up for days. When they closed up at night, we'd be there waiting, and we'd follow them home. They didn't live too far away. They lived in an apartment building that also had a doctor's office. We walked behind them and said things to scare them. One night, we rang the bell to the doctor's office, and he pressed the buzzer to let us in. When he did, we waited under the stairwell until we heard the door to his office close. Then we went upstairs to the Polish family's apartment, took their boots from their doorway, and threw them out into the snow. I hated myself for what I was doing, but I could not stop. Most of the time, I had a razor blade with me; so before I went home, I would cut myself. That was my punishment for what I was putting those people through.

I did not know how hard it was on them. They had no choice except to take court action against us, me and Crystal. When we went to court, one of the officers saw the cuts on my arms and told the judge. I was sent to the Metropolitan State Hospital for thirty days' observation, and Crystal went to a school for wayward girls. That is how it all began.

That hospital stay was a traumatic time for me. I remember sitting on the bed waiting to be admitted. I was wearing nothing more than a thin johnny, and the room was freezing. I lay my head on the pillow with my feet hanging over the side of the bed. As I waited, I looked at the walls; they were made of cinder blocks, painted gray. It was an eerie feeling. Finally, I was admitted and brought to a ward where patients were locked in. There were also seclusion rooms where I'd be sent if I cut myself. Each day when I saw the doctor, he would ask me questions. I do not think I answered one question that he asked me. I didn't talk to anyone.

During those thirty days, I had to see a doctor every day. My mother came to visit; we never talked about what I was doing to myself. It was out in the open now, yet we did not discuss it. My two sisters also visited. We did not discuss my self-injury either. In fact, we spent our time discussing the problems of the other patients in the ward. (Years later, they told me they did not think there was anything wrong with me; they thought I was doing it for attention.) My sisters asked me what was wrong with everyone on the ward because I talked to the patients more than I talked to anyone else. I wouldn't even talk to the nurses. I hated that place, and sometimes I would find something sharp and cut myself.

When it came to the judicial system, I realized just how naïve my parents really were, being from the old country. My parents believed that just because people were educated and had power, whatever they said was right. They didn't question the judge's decision. I never blamed my parents; they did the best they could. I know they loved me even though they found the words hard to say. Some Irish people are like that; they love but do not know how to get close. For some reason, they cannot open their arms and hold you.

When the thirty days were up, I had to return to court. The doctor's report recommended that I be transferred to Massachusetts Mental Health in Boston. This hospital was closer to home and had a larger staff with more young girls as patients.

The second night I was there, I got out of bed at two o'clock in the morning. I went to the sunroom, which was surrounded by windows. I sat down and put my feet up on the windowsill. I cannot tell you what came over me, but I put my foot through one window then stood up and just kept putting my fists through the windows. I could not stop. The nurses' station was a distance away, so by the time they arrived, I had broken quite a few windows. My hands were cut so badly that I needed many stitches. When they got through with me, they put me in a room by myself so they could keep an eye on me. That was the worst I had felt in a long time. I remember feeling as though I didn't want to live anymore. I felt very bad about the effect my childhood prank had on some very nice people. I was ashamed and so very, very lonely. I felt I was no good and so dirty. I hated myself so much that I kept to myself most of the time.

I felt bad about myself for a long time. One night, I was sitting in my pajamas after coming back from listening to one of the nurses play the piano. She was very talented, and I remember she played "Some Enchanted Evening." I loved that song, but it put me in a sad mood. I set fire to my pajamas with a book of matches I had found. My roommate witnessed the event and called for help immediately. The nurses grabbed me and threw a blanket over me. I was okay. That was the first and last time I ever did that.

I met a few young girls like myself. These girls were also around sixteen, and I remember one girl in particular. She was very small and had red hair. Once in a while, she would put her hand through a window, but the biggest thing I remember her doing seemed rather strange to me. She had a thing about her belly button; she stuck things into it. When the nursing staff found out what she was doing, she had to be treated; and when she came back to the ward, she was kept in her room with a nursing staff around the clock. After a few days, I asked if she was feeling better and if I could visit with her. The nurse told me it was fine to visit now. When I saw her, I asked what she was doing to herself and what had she put in her belly button. She said that there had been several things, but the last thing was a piece of glass, and it had gotten infected. With that, she pulled up her pajama top and showed me her belly button.

Honestly, I got sick to my stomach when I saw how sore and red it looked. I asked her if it had hurt and how she could possibly do this to herself, and she answered, "Well, how can you cut yourself?" That shut me right up. At that time in my life, I believed that everyone who was self-abusing must be cutting. I didn't realize that people did all kinds of things to themselves—hair pulling, fingernail and toenail pulling, cutting, head banging, burning, etc.

There were four of us who hung out together. We all liked to draw and paint. While we were at a meeting one morning with the staff, I asked the doctor if they would give us a room to ourselves where we could go and be left alone to just draw and play cards and other games. He said that he would think it over. For the next few meetings, I continued to bring up the subject of this special room. He said he was hesitant because he was afraid we would use the room for the wrong reasons. He was afraid that we would break the windows and cut ourselves if left alone.

I assured him that I would not do anything to myself in the room, and that if I felt the need to hurt myself, I would come out of the room. He made us agree to leave the door unlocked at all times and informed us that the nurses would come by periodically, knock on the door, and come in to check up on us. We made all kinds of promises, and he finally broke down and agreed to give us the room. It was great; they got us all kinds of drawing materials and paints.

I believe we had that room for a few months, during which time two of the girls were discharged. Helen and I were the only two remaining, and we got real antsy. We were bored and wanted to do something different. So we decided to climb up on the windowsill, open the window, which only opened from the top about four inches, and drop jars of red and yellow finger paints down to the street. We counted to three, let go, and away they went. What a splash they made on the street. The colors looked great all splattered together. Little did we know that street painting would become a big hit in the eighties. We knew we were in trouble when the nurse came running through the door, telling us to get down and to get out of the room. She locked the room right away and called for the doctor. It took a while for him to come up to the ward, and we both just sat there waiting. Every now and then, we would look at each other and laugh, saying it was worth it since the street looked great. Well, of course, we lost the use of the room.

After a few months, I begged the doctor to let me go home for a weekend. He agreed only if I promised not to cut myself. And that if I felt like I was going to harm myself, I had to come back to the hospital. I agreed and was permitted to go home. I loved going home, but I also looked forward to going back to the hospital because I felt safe there; and if I abused myself, there was someone there to take care of me; my family did not have to see what I did to myself. Also, I was with other kids who were doing the same thing, so I guess it was a form of fitting in. It sure beat sitting in a cold hallway or out in a field somewhere then going home and trying to hide it from the world.

Finally, I left that hospital and went home. It was good for a while. Then I started to drink again. I went back to the Spa, but this time, I was bringing the bottle of whiskey in with me and putting it in my Coke.

I went back to the restaurant next door that was run by the Polish family and apologized for behaving so badly—banging on their window, following them home, and throwing their shoes into the snow. I told them I would never do anything like that again. They were very kind to me and said they were very sorry to have called the police, but they didn't know how far I would go. They thought I was going to end up breaking the front window of the store. I assured them that they had nothing to fear from me. I would never hurt them or their store. We all ended up being friends. And later, after I got married and had my son, my sister and I would go in for lunch with our children. The daughter would hold my son and warm his bottle on her stove.

At that time I had a new friend, Joanne, and one night we went drinking. Drinking was a big thing in the fifties—it seemed like everyone drank. After drinking, we went back to her house, and I went into her bathroom and got one of her father's razor blades. I told Joanne that I didn't feel very well and that I was going to go out onto the front porch and sit for a while. I sat there for a while, and a lonely feeling came over me. Even though my friend was just inside and we were good friends, I found I couldn't talk to her like I had been able to talk to Crystal. I felt like I had to cut myself, but this time, it was my face. I cut my forehead so badly that Joanne had to call an ambulance.

They needed to stitch both inside and outside of the skin because the cut was so deep. I remember, as I was lying there, all the clamps they had to use all over my face. They were very good to me, and I believe they took into consideration that I was a girl because today you can barely see the scar.

Chapter Eight

From that hospital, I was sent to Boston State Hospital. This is where the story of my real survival begins. This was the beginning of years of struggle and turmoil and learning how one can fall through the cracks—not only in the school system but in state-run hospitals as well.

As I remember the hospital, it had six floors and was called the Reception Building. Entering through the front door, the office was on the right; that is where everyone was instructed to report in, letting the staff know where they were going. On the left was the elevator with a stairwell to the side. Each area of the hospital was given a number, such as Reception One, which was an open ward, meaning that the patients could come and go as they pleased. Some Reception One patients actually worked outside the hospital during the day and reported back at night. Those patients would soon be discharged. Across the hall was Reception Two and so on up to the third floor. On the second and third floors, the wards were locked. The third floor was Reception Five. Reception Five was where patients who were considered very bad were sent. The men were housed on the left side and the women on the right. This is where I was eventually put.

Being this young girl with all kinds of energy and not knowing what to do with myself, I began to act up the first chance I got. If I wasn't cutting myself, I was acting like a clown and getting into trouble that way.

I found myself very attracted to one of the head nurses—still confused about such feelings, thinking it was so wrong and dirty but having them nonetheless. I just stuffed the feelings down deep and turned to self-hatred. I would cut myself very deeply, punishing myself for those feelings and trying to make them go away. I never felt able to talk about such things to anyone. All I could think was, *My god, I could be a lesbian*, and the thought was slowly killing me.

It was very important for the staff to try to make Reception One look like a palace as it was the first area anyone, visitors included, would see upon entering Boston State Hospital. One of the nurses brought in a different chair every week to place in the reception area; some furniture was donated, and to me, it all looked like it had been dug out of the trash.

One day, the nurses decided to have a painting party to further dress up the room. The head nurse, who I had the crush on, put on a state dress (used on patients when they were sent to the seclusion room) and asked if I would help out. I'd have done anything to get her attention, so of course, I agreed. As usual, I ended up doing something really stupid. While she was up on a chair, painting the wall, I turned to load up my roller with paint and, turning back toward her, proceeded to roll the paint up the back of her dress. The state dresses were so heavy I knew the paint would not go through to her uniform. Needless to say, I bypassed Reception Three and was sent straight up to Reception Five.

It was when I arrived at Reception Five that I met the head nurse, Barbara McInnis. I remember seeing her out on the grounds; she was a heavyset nurse, and I always thought she looked so serious and quiet. Come to find out, she was an angel. That day, Barbara took me into the four-bed dorm where I would be sleeping. She told me to sit on my bed and said she'd be right back. She came back in with a tall black girl whom she introduced as Dotty, and then she left us alone to talk.

Dotty sat on the bed across from me, and we talked for a long time. Then she rested her arms on her legs and turned them over so her wrists were facing up and said, "I cut myself also." I remember looking down at her arms, and all I could see were white lines from her wrists to her elbows. There wasn't room for another cut. Dotty talked a little about some of the reasons why she cut herself, and as time went on and we became closer, she confided in me about her abuse from a family member. I won't go into details. I remember feeling so bad for what she'd gone through. Over time, Dotty and I became as close as sisters. We stayed in touch after we left the hospital for the longest time, and then we drifted apart. We both stayed in touch with Barbara McInnis, the nurse who had more insight, understanding, and compassion for the two young girls who were so lost back then. I will carry the memory of Barbara and Dotty for the rest of my life.

Letter from Barbara McInnis: Memories of Boston State Hospital and of Connie

> As a young nurse, new grad 1956, I had my first job at Boston State Hospital. It was a wonderful time to be there because people were benefiting with the new medications that were now available, like thorazine. It was considered the new wonder drug for the [illegible] women and mental illness.

In general the philosophy of a state hospital then was to provide a safe environment for the patients and staff. In general the professional staff was physicians, nurses, social workers, and occasionally chaplains. Each professional group also had students in their area rotating through for 2 to 3 months at a time. The nonprofessional staff were called attendants and were usually high school grads with on-the-job training or college students studying for work as psychologists.

As in any human service department staff were different in their responses and outlooks on life. The hard-nosed, tough employee looked at every bit of negative behavior as a threat to them personally or a way to upset other patients on the ward. If this happened that staff would then be blamed for losing control and it would show up on their employment record. So these folks ruled with a heavy hand and used many methods to control the behavior of the patients. Because they were so controlling they were the first staff to think of using physical force, restraints and seclusion. Very often they would not know what to say themselves—staffpeople saw this only in terms of their personal behavior—and how if a patient injured themselves, they would get written up and be blamed for it. Usually the staff who were so controlling and inflexible were fearful for their personal safety, unable to be empathetic and aware of the patients' personal feelings.

Many of the controlling staff came from controlling and punitive families and it was the only way they knew how to respond. These were the staff that resorted to physical restraint and seclusion, and as meds became more available they used a lot of chemical restraint (meds). For them it would never occur to them to help a patient talk it out.

The next group of people were [liberals] who saw their job as being there for the patient. Trying to understand any negative behavior, letting a patient talk about feelings, finding ways to safely let a patient use negative energy in such a way so as not to hurt themselves, i.e., games, dancing, singing, going for walks and talking alone of in groups.

Another group of staff came from a background of people that were accustomed to help people who needed it. Some of this staff, this group, was most interesting because they were so loving and caring to the patients, the patients loved them and did not want anyone else to care for them. Many patients got well faster under the care of such kind staff. This staff found it difficult to set and enforce limits of any kind—they were constantly criticized by physicians and hospital administrators.

Another group of staff were people that were rejects from getting jobs as policemen or firemen or prison guards and they tended to be harsh combative folks who were overzealous in their control methods.

With so many various groups of staffpeople who had different philosophical ideas, each group believed they had the only correct way to do things. Staff reactions to a patient's behavior depended each day on what staffpeople were there.

[illegible line] for meds, this in turn was interpreted and given by the nurses. The doctor would often [illegible] for suggestions on how to control behavior, i.e., seclusion, [illegible] tubs, or going to occupational therapy, leaving the ward to go for a walk. However many of the staff worked there longer than the physicians so staff took it upon themselves to ignore what the doctor wrote for "[illegible] therapy" and did what they thought was best. Physicians came as medical students, residents, interns and fellows. They changed monthly to yearly so a lot of the attendants and nurses feel they know more about the patients than the docs do so physicians' orders are compromised.

In terms of self-abuse patients: Mostly back then they were seen as character disorders or people who acted out when under the influence of alcohol. Again some staff were compassionate while others—who did not understand it and who were threatened themselves when people started to cut themselves up (staff from controlling backgrounds or who unconsciously had thoughts of doing the same thing)—were quick to use restraints and seclusion for this problem. The hospital policy was to "keep patients and staff safe."

When I look back on the professional behavior of my colleagues I see that we all did what we believed was the best for the patient. Except for assault and battery by a staff person to a patient there was no right or wrong way to care for people. Battery was definitely considered wrong by all except in cases of self-protection.

My memory of Connie in those early days is that when she displayed uncooperative behavior it was to keep staff away from her. When she started to cut herself up it created more distance between Connie and others. Fear in not knowing what to say or do next to help Connie. Most people saw this behavior in terms of secondary acting out because of substance abuse. Often staff would label Connie as a trouble maker, looking at her behavior in terms of the trouble it caused them rather than being able to see it as representative of her personal feelings about herself. Staff saw Connie as having problems varying from simple schizophrenic—manic to character disorder/substance abuse, to troubled adolescent who wants to have her own way.

I saw Connie's behavior as representative of the inner pain and hurt she was in at that time. I saw her behavior more as cause and effect. Someone hurt Connie and she responded with negative behavior. Everything for her was a calamity and chaos. Her psyche seldom allowed her peacefulness.

Years later when I found out that Connie had a literacy problem that she successfully concealed I wondered how many other things in her life were hidden and pushed deep into her subconscious mind. I had an analogy for Connie. Like smoke and fire and when there is a lot of smoke there is a lot of fire. I saw her distressing behavior as a plea for help, and when she hurt herself a lot physically and emotionally I figured there was tremendous pain and suffering going on inside. Connie was always clever so this combined with her made her a person easily misunderstood, because the message that she sent out was "don't mess with me," and it caused distancing and isolation, which was the opposite of what she really needed.

Whenever some staffperson did or said something to degrade or humiliate Connie it was because they were unable to know the effect it would have. Staff had no idea it would injure Connie further.

When I met Connie she was able to communicate to me that she was sensitive and hurting a lot and she tried to keep these feelings to herself. She hid them by her [illegible] tough act in her behavior. My style of working was to offer people the compassion that I felt in hopes that other staff would see the wisdom in what I did. This was not always so. Some staffpeople worked following their own philosophies.

Barbara McGinnis

Just a Name

The story of my life; pencil me in, erase me out.

I see your eraser being pushed and pulled quickly across my

name, with little pieces of eraser getting embedded in the fibers

of the paper as my name seemingly fades away.

Either your lips blow me softly off the paper, or your baby finger

swipes me to one side, then to the floor.

Look closely. You will never be able to completely erase me.

At Least Not Yet!

That was the way my life felt to me: almost invisible and certainly not important to anyone, not even myself.

Not all of the people who worked in these mental hospitals were bad, but I came in contact with many who used their position to take advantage of the patients. It was a power trip for some of them, an open door to sexual advances for others.

I ran away from Boston State Hospital to go visit a student nurse in Salem, Massachusetts, at the hospital where she was studying. Back then, we didn't think twice about hitching a ride with a stranger, so that is how I got there. I went up to the dorm where she was staying. She didn't know I was coming, so it was a surprise to her when I arrived. She let me come up to her room, and we talked for a long time. Then she said I had to go back to the hospital. I cried and told her I didn't want to go back, and she pleaded with me. I decided to just leave and told her I would be fine. I just wanted to go for a walk. She asked me to wait in her room for a moment. I know she was aware that if I left, I would cut myself. She called the police. When they got there, she told me she was very sorry but that was what she had to do. She knew I was not going back to the hospital voluntarily. The police took me to Danvers State Hospital. That is the hospital where the old movie *The Snake Pit* was filmed.

I had to stay at Danvers for two weeks because of the paperwork involved to get me back to Boston State. That place was one hellhole. I had never seen such sick people in my life.

At Danvers State Hospital, as you entered the ward, there was a long hallway with beds all in a row against the wall. At night, they would bring out a tray of sandwiches, cut in half, made with mint jelly. The food there was absolutely horrible. I couldn't bring myself to eat the meals they served, so I would wait for the sandwiches at night. By that time, I was so hungry, anything would have tasted good. Today, I can't even look at a jar of mint jelly.

I never went outside even when they would gather up some of the patients to go for a walk around the grounds. The days were always cloudy, and it seemed to rain almost every night while I was there. Watching TV was not one of my favorite things to do, but everyone there gathered around the TV, and some would even talk to it. Some patients would just stare and rock back and forth in their chairs as though they were looking straight through everyone. I don't know how anyone could concentrate on a program with all the chattering going on in the room. Believe me, it was one scary and very depressing place to be; the people were very sick, and I believe, many of the staff had mental problems as well.

No one was allowed to lie on their bed during the day. If you tried to lie down and an attendant came by, he would take his stick (which looked like a club with keys attached) and hit the iron part of the bed. He would yell at the patients to get off the beds. I felt so bad for some of those poor people; many were so drugged from the Thorazine, they had trouble staying upright. It bothered me when the attendants did this, especially to the older patients; the attendants seemed to take pleasure in startling them. Some patients would start to cry, and others would beg to be allowed to rest for just a little while. The attendants made them sit upright in chairs. I can still see their heads bobbing up and down as they tried to stay awake. How sad to be that medicated and not allowed to rest. What the hell was the staff thinking?

I don't know why Thorazine was not more regulated. If those patients had been given less, maybe they wouldn't be so tired. I think that once the doctor wrote the order for medications, he never saw the patient again. If he did, it was to spend five minutes with him or her; then he was gone for the day, never knowing what was going on after he left. Or did he know?

I spent most of my time sitting on the windowsill. I guess being so close to the outside made me feel far away from the madness.

During my various hospital stays, I was approached on three different occasions by women staff members. All of this served to confuse me further.

One night, I found a piece of glass under a radiator; it had fallen there after a patient broke a window. I picked it up and waited until everyone was in bed. I sat in the day hall with all the lights out and just started to cut. The cuts were very deep. I sat there for what must have been two hours when all of a sudden, the lights went on. I was huddled way over in a corner, and a nurse came over and asked me if I was all right. I said I was just fine; I just couldn't sleep. I hoped she would leave me alone.

She started to walk toward me and saw the blood. She called for another nurse, and they took me to the treatment room. One of the doctors stitched me up and told the nurse he wanted me to sleep in a bed outside the nurses' station so they could keep an eye on me. By that time, I was so tired and so sore I didn't care where they put me. I remember that one nurse was quite big and looked like a man. She came out of the office quite a bit to see how I was doing. She would rub my back and ask what made me do that to myself. I really didn't want to talk, but I told her I didn't know why I did it. She rubbed my back some more and said she'd be back later. Something didn't feel right to me, so I couldn't sleep.

Sure enough, she came back out and started to rub my back again. She began to put her hands under my pajamas and rub my sides, and then she moved her hand around the front and started to put her hand on my breast. I quickly turned over and pushed my arms real close to my sides so she could not fit her hands there again. I was scared; I didn't know what was going on. I had never been approached by a woman before. I told her I was really tired and asked her to please leave me alone. I told her she didn't have to worry about me cutting myself again. I just wanted to be left alone. She said, "Okay, I'll let you get some sleep," and went back to her office. I never told anyone what had happened. I felt that I was the dirty one and that it was my fault because I had let her rub my back. Well, who wouldn't? It had felt so good after feeling so bad. Now it was all bad again!

Chapter Nine

Finally, it was time to be transferred back to Boston State Hospital. First, I want you to know that I was not mentally ill. I was very aware of what was going on in these places. I saw a lot of patients get roughed up. They were very sick, and they couldn't speak up for themselves. If they did, no one believed them. I became very strong; being so young, I felt somewhat safe there. I even went to work from that hospital each day and, after work, would return to the hospital. It seemed that all the nurses knew I didn't belong there, except for the cutting I was doing sometimes. I just didn't have the confidence to do anything better with myself.

I used to go home for the weekends; sometimes I would come back okay, and sometimes I would come back early because I had cut myself again. Many times, the staff didn't even know that I had cut myself. One night, when I returned early and was getting ready for bed, I asked a nurse if I could sit on the back patio; it was especially hot in the hospital that evening. The nurse agreed, and after I seated myself on the patio, an attendant came out and pulled up a chair. She was a black woman, married, with a son. She was one of the nicest people there, and she was a very nice-looking woman. We had become good friends because she didn't treat me like a patient. She asked me if I would like to meet with her the next time I went home for the weekend. I said that would be nice. She got up and put her hands on my shoulders and squeezed them very lightly. Then she bent down and whispered to me that she would be right back with her phone number. When she handed it to me, she told me not to tell anyone because she would be fired. I promised her I wouldn't tell. We sat there for a while longer and talked. I really liked talking to her. Her voice was so soothing; it seemed to make me tired. Finally, I went to bed.

The next time I went home, I called, and we met at a restaurant near her home. It was a very nice place. She told me that she wanted to treat me to dinner. I was about seventeen at this time, but being so tall, I looked older. When my friend ordered a drink, the waiter turned to me and asked me what I would like. I felt good because I could pass for twenty-one, so I took a deep breath and said, "I'll have a beer please." When he walked away, I asked her why he hadn't asked for my license or identification, and she agreed that I looked older than I really was. We had a few drinks, and I was starting to feel relaxed. After dinner, we had another drink. I excused myself to use the ladies' room and went into the stall.

Then I heard her come into the ladies' room. When I came out, she took my hand and said she thought I was a really good-looking girl. I said, "Are you crazy? I'm a mess." I didn't feel at all pretty. I thought she was just trying to make me feel good about myself. When I started to walk away, she nudged me and said she really meant it. Then she leaned forward to kiss me. I turned my cheek to her, but she turned and kissed me on the lips. I didn't say anything to her; I just walked back to the table. When she got back, she said she was very sorry that she had done that; she didn't know what made her do it, and it would never happen again. She said that she'd had too much to drink and was truly sorry. I believed her and said, "Okay." I never did understand where she was coming from that night. She was a very attractive woman with a husband and son. Why would she do something like that? I buried that memory also.

Now that I am older and wiser, I really believe she felt ashamed for what she'd done. I saw a lot more of her in the hospital, and she never approached me sexually again. That led me to believe that she was sorry for the incident, and I forgive her today.

It is much easier for a woman to have close friends than it is for a man. Women can hug and kiss, and that's okay; but let a man do it, and he feels that he has lost his manhood and that other men will call him gay, especially when they are young. A lot of men have best friends who they love, but you will seldom see them hug or kiss each other. What a shame to have to hide their feelings when it is much better to be open and tell your friends what you feel. We all like to hear that we are loved, no matter who says it.

At the hospital, I believe that some of those attendants had a lot of their own problems. I think that by working in those hospitals, they felt better about themselves. I don't think they set out to hurt anyone, but they were dealing with their own issues; and when someone like me came along, they could see that I was basically okay and able to talk to them. When I was eighteen, I started to really talk with people; I mean talk like an adult. I would get them to open up to me, and it was as though I was the one working there and they were the patients. It was quite strange.

The third and last woman at Boston State to approach me, strangely enough, lived in the same neighborhood. She asked me to call her when I came home from the hospital on weekends. I never gave it any thought because I always enjoyed talking with her, and she with me. She was also married and had children in high school and college. One night, I happened to go out with a friend; and of course, we went for a few drinks. I was on my way home, and I thought I would give her a call; I never felt much like going home after drinking. She answered the phone, and her voice was so soft. I told her I was up the street and on my way home and asked if she wanted to meet and talk. She said that her husband and children were gone for the weekend and asked me if I would like to come to her house. I asked if she had anything there to drink, and she replied, "Yes, of course." I headed for her house.

When I got there, we went into the living room. The television was on, and the lights were very low. I sat on a chair, and she on the couch. We talked for a while, and she brought me a beer. I don't know what she was drinking, but I know it was strong: I could smell it. After a while, she asked if I would like some music. She knew I liked music because at the hospital, I always had a radio on. I said, "Sure." She got up and turned the stereo on and asked me if I wanted another drink. Of course I did! When she came back from the kitchen, she sat on the couch with both drinks and made a gesture for me to sit beside her. I did, but I sat at the other end of the couch. She kept telling me how smart I was and that I did not belong at that hospital and that I should stop hurting myself—I was too nice a person to do that to myself. Back then, I did not like to hear those words because I did not think I was a good person; I truly hated myself. These people could not understand that.

When I think back, they were seeing the person I am today. It is so sad that I had to go through years of feeling bad about myself.

As we sat and talked, I got her to talk about herself and her husband. She told me that she was not in love with him anymore and that they were staying together because of the children. I could not understand that at all, but now I do. Again, she asked me if I would like another drink. I was really feeling good by then, very comfortable, so I said, "Sure." When she came back, she had on only her slip. I was a little surprised until she said she just had to get out of her clothes, and her slip was her nightgown. We talked some more, but I was starting to feel that I had done something wrong. I felt kind of sad. I put my face in my hands and started to cry. I can't remember what we were talking about that made me feel so sad. She pulled me toward her and put her arm around me and started rubbing my head.

I remember how good it felt to have someone hold me, but I knew again that there was something very wrong about this. No matter how good it felt, I couldn't stay there. I told her I was all right and that I had to get home.

We both got up, and she walked me to the door. She said she was glad that I had called and that I could call anytime. With that, she went to hug me, and I pulled away and walked out the door. I just could not let anyone get that close to me. I never believed people when they told me how nice I was. I always felt bad and dirty and that they were lying to me and didn't really mean what they were saying. I still, to this day, cannot figure out what they were thinking—why they needed me to be close to them. I do believe that the last two women were very lonely and did like to be with me. All three women took advantage of me and their positions at the hospital, and it left me with a bad feeling. As always, I thought I was doing something wrong.

When you're young like I was, you don't always know what is right and wrong. The first one of the three women was definitely gay; she went too far and left me feeling rotten. How dare she do something like that to me! I am sure she must have touched other patients as well. It is very hard to understand why those people took such terrible advantage of patients. I know it must still go on today.

Chapter Ten

In 1959 while I was a patient at Boston State Hospital and only sixteen years of age, I witnessed many patients before and after they had shock treatments. The shock room (as the patients called it) was located across from the arts and crafts room. The art room had cracks in the walls and cinder blocks painted a dingy gray. When I think back, I recall the paintings and drawings hung on the walls to cover the cracks.

I would be so wrapped up in what I was drawing that every time a nurse brought a patient to the shock room, usually hitting the wall with the gurney, I would jump. I can clearly recall the faces on those patients as they lay strapped down on a gurney, the black rubber mouthpiece positioned between their teeth, waiting for their turn. It was so sad for me to watch those poor souls, some just lying there and others moaning and weeping softly to themselves. Although electroshock therapy has been used since the 1930s, it has left many patients helpless and dysfunctional.

There were many patients at Boston State who were put in the seclusion room. Some of them were so out of control that they would not only hurt themselves but put the other patients in danger as well. The staff used Thorazine on some of the worst patients, and it would knock them out. When they woke up, they were like zombies; they didn't even know what day it was or where they were. One patient was so doped up from the Thorazine that she put her hand on the radiator (it was terribly hot) and got the biggest blister on the palm of her hand. I remember watching her hold her hand and rocking back and forth in her chair. I went over to her and took her hand to see how badly she was burned; it was awful. I was a little scared of her because she was a big girl and tended to lose control sometimes, but I decided to get a cold washcloth and try to at least help her control the pain. I told her it would make her hand feel so much better and asked if I could put it on. She looked so sad and just nodded her head yes. She didn't talk much, but she put out her hand and let me wrap the cloth around it. I continued doing this for several days. After that, every time she walked past me, she would show me her hand and smile. I believe that was her way of saying thank-you.

I am not sure how long the doctors had to do their internships there, but it seemed like the doctors were changed frequently; there was a new one every time I turned around. There was the doctor who gave the order that if my friend Dotty or I cut ourselves, we were to be given a shot of Thorazine and then put in the seclusion room. Well, I can tell you, I soon found out what all those other patients felt like. It was like I had cement shoes on, and I just didn't want to walk anywhere. I remember they made me walk to the cafeteria, and it seemed like it was a hundred-mile trek. After I finally got there, I didn't even have the energy to pick up a fork and eat. Then I had the long walk back to the ward. I just fell into bed and slept for hours. It was the worst feeling in the world.

When my mother and sisters visited me, I made them promise never to let the doctors do electroshock therapy on me. I don't know if they had ever given it a thought, but it scared me so much that I told my dad about it and about other things the doctors did to the patients, hoping he would make sure it never happened to me. I know now that the doctors pretty much did whatever they wanted to keep the patients quiet.

Not all of the staff was that bad; one nurse in particular stands out as being very warm, caring, and special. On this one occasion, I had cut myself, and the head nurse told me she had to give me a shot of Thorazine. I pleaded with her not to do it, and instead, she walked me to the seclusion room and said, "If you will sit here and take these newspapers and rip them up, I will leave the door open and not give you a shot." She left for a short while; and when she returned, she came into the room, sat on the rubber mattress with me, and asked if I wanted to talk. We talked for a while, and I really did feel better. We ultimately became good friends and stayed in touch. She left the hospital, and in later years, we ended up working at the same nursing home together. She and her mother attended my wedding, and her mom gave my son his very first pair of shoes. Barbara had a huge impact on me and my life. She is a terrific person, and I love her so much for seeing the real me. Thanks, Barbara!

When I was around the student nurses, they made me feel good about myself. They gave me the feeling that they really cared, and I believe it had something to do with the fact that we were so close in age. I so looked forward to the day shift when they would be on duty, and I could spend time around them and feel good about myself. At the end of the day, when they left, I found myself right back in the hellhole of my feelings.

We had ward meetings every week. The nurses would come around to each bed area and yell, "Come on, everyone, out in the day hall!" They would round us just like cattle. I can still see some of the patients walking so close to the walls that it looked like the walls were holding them up. Because I hated to go to these meetings, I was the last to arrive. The doctor had everyone pull their chairs into a circle, and he'd sit with a clipboard in his lap. A couple of the head nurses sat on either side of him like he was some kind of king with his harem. Scattered among the patients were some of the student nurses who spent a few hours a day on our ward.

If any of the patients got up and tried to leave, a nurse would jump right up and make them sit back down. Some of the patients got so bad that they just couldn't sit there; they had to get up and walk around, not only because of their illness but because of the medications they had been given. In my mind's eye, I can still see the student nurse (just a kid herself) trying to talk a patient into sitting down. Her voice was so soft she was barely heard over the chattering in the room. But she stayed with her even when the patient became agitated and started raising her voice; she just walked around the room with her until the meeting was over. She was so young but so caring.

At the meetings, I always moved my chair back away from the circle. For some reason, it seemed to bother the doctor that I wasn't right in line with the others. He would motion to the nurse, and she'd say, "Pull your chair up, Connie." Why it was such a big deal, I don't know. I was more comfortable sitting where I was. Being the brat I was back then, I would try to piss them off by turning my chair around with my back to them. They finally decided that having me face forward was the better option, so they told me if I turned my chair around, I could sit where I wanted. I was angry that I was being treated as a "mental patient." I never viewed myself that way.

I never spoke during the meetings. I just sat and observed what was going on. Then one day, and I still smile about this, the doctor asked a patient if she had anything she would like to talk about. She jumped right up and said, "I sure do!" She was really mad, and in a loud voice, she said, "No one cares about the birds. It is very cold out, and they don't have anything to eat!"

The doctor just said, "Okay, Mary, sit down."

He tried to move on to the next patient, but Mary was not to be quieted so easily. She jumped back up once more and, standing in the middle of the circle, said in a very loud voice, "No one gives a damn about the birds." The doctor again tried to calm her and asked her to please sit down.

With that, I stood up and asked the doctor, "Have you ever been in the patient's cafeteria? You should see all the bread that is being wasted! The patients get bread with every meal, and more than half of us don't even eat it, so just give her some to feed the damn birds!" I shoved my chair back and left the room. They never bothered coming after me; they knew I would not come back to the meeting.

Today, when I think of that moment, I picture the woman (before she got so sick) getting up each morning and feeding the birds before she left for work. I think that the staff lost sight of the fact that we all had lives before the hospital. The doctors treated us like case files; and to the rest of the staff, we were just patients, mostly treated like caged animals.

I don't want you to think that all of the staff were bad. I remember being in a locked ward where we'd have to ask permission to go downstairs to the Coke machine; then we were only given permission if we had ground privileges. Sometimes the attendants would leave the door open for better ventilation, and they'd sit by it so we didn't escape. Some of the patients would try to run out; but the attendant would just put his foot up, across the opening, and block their exit.

One day, I felt pretty bad and just wanted to get out and run around. I waited until the nurse, who was sitting by the open door, started talking to another patient; and I made a beeline for the opening. I just kept running, right down the stairs and out the front door. Before I knew it, there were two nurses and one attendant chasing me down the street. I ran up another street; but when I looked back, they were almost right alongside of me, so I headed straight out into the traffic. There was a car coming toward me, but at that moment, I really didn't care if I got killed. The car hit me, and I went up onto the hood and down onto the street. I was not hurt that badly, just some cuts and bruises, and I had to wear a sling on my arm for a while. It was just one of those times that I didn't care what happened to me. Needless to say, I was not allowed off the locked ward for a long time afterward.

I remember far too many days and nights spent in that horrible seclusion room. As time went by, I dreaded it more and more. Sometimes I would refuse to go in for the nurses; I would plead with them to please let me go back to my room and sit quietly on my bed, and I would promise not to cut myself anymore. I felt just like a little kid who had misbehaved. As hard as I pleaded, they insisted that I had no choice. It really made me mad because I hadn't hurt anyone but myself, and yet I was being punished.

On one occasion, I was quite desperate. I was pleading with the nurses when I looked down the hall; and there, just turning the corner, were three very tall men in white suits. One of the nurses had put a call into the male ward for them to send help over to get me into the seclusion room. As they got closer, I felt my heart pounding; it was like I was going into battle. I remember noticing how they swung their keys around as they headed toward me; I could see the power trip reflected in their eyes, and they knew I was aware of it.

But I stood my ground, scared but feeling brave at the same time. It seemed that they took pleasure in being rough with me. Nine out of every ten male attendants that I came in contact with me during my hospital stays loved the power they had and were far from gentle with the patients. They twisted my arm so far up toward my back that I thought it was going to break. Then one of them grabbed me by the hair and pushed me down while another held my feet and planted his knee sharply on my back. They pushed my face into the hot black rubber mattress on the floor. They finally said that they would let me up if I promised to calm down. What choice did I have?

Finally, they left the seclusion room to stand guard outside while a nurse made me strip down and put on what they called a state dress, sort of like a heavy potato sack. Most of the nurses where aware of my modesty and were decent enough to turn their backs while I disrobed. The nurse would then check the inside of my mouth to be sure I wasn't stashing any glass there. The door was locked, and as they walked away, I could hear them whispering and giggling.

The sound of the door locking rang out loudly down the hallway, and I was left in the bare, hot room. I curled up in the corner and tried to understand why they were doing this to me. Why did they have to be so rough? They always made me feel worse about myself than I already did. Why were they punishing me for hurting myself? As much as I wanted to cry, the tears remained in my throat. Back then, I really had a hard time crying. It was the one thing I refused to do. Maybe if I had just let go of the tears, I would have felt a lot better.

Hours would pass in that room before anyone came back to check on me. If I had the misfortune of being put in the seclusion room at night, I was left there until the 7 a.m. shift came. I would have to yell so hard and so long for anyone to hear me, just to get some water or use the bathroom. Believe me, the heat was never regulated in that room, and it was hot as hell! It was the loneliest feeling in the world, being locked in there; and sometimes I would pray that if I fell asleep, I would never wake up.

For the life of me, I could not understand the logic behind the way we were treated. They said the seclusion room was not punishment but only a way to prevent us from hurting ourselves again. But that never made any sense because they knew that once we had cut, we were not going to do it again for at least a few days.

Today, I understand the difference in the way we were treated on the day shift versus the night shift. During the day shift, there was a head nurse and a registered nurse (RN) in charge of the ward. There were female attendants and at least four or five student nurses. Each student nurse had a patient as a case study and was expected to write a paper at the end of her three-month rotation. Therefore, she would go out of her way to spend time talking to that patient, hoping to gain insight into the problem they had, and trying to make them feel better.

The head nurse on my ward was Barbara McInnis. She was great and always tried her best not to lock me in the seclusion room. She made a pact with me that I was to go into the room, leave the door open, and sit on the mattress, and rip up paper or magazines. She would sit with me and do the same. When I wanted a drink of water or to use the bathroom, I was permitted to go, unsupervised, but had to come right back and stay there until I felt better. She actually left the decision up to me as to when I was okay, but we agreed that it would be at least one hour. When I got back to my own room, she would even drop by and talk with me for a while. I always stayed in the seclusion room for at least an hour when Barbara was there because she treated me so well and showed me that she trusted what I said about not hurting myself again right away.

Then the night shift—which consisted of only three female attendants, no head nurse, and no student nurses—would come on duty with their knitting and books. They seemed to be more interested in what they were working on than what we were doing or needed. There was a night supervisor who came through the ward twice each night, once to give medications and the second time to just check up on the attendants. This supervisor had six wards to keep up with, and there was always some kind of confusion, so she spent a lot of time running around.

Because the night staff was more interested in their own thing, they didn't like their routine to be altered in any way. If I hurt myself, it meant that I was disturbing them, so their answer was to shove me into the seclusion room at the end of the hall where no one had to deal with me for the remainder of the night. There, I would stay until morning, and they went back to their knitting and books. When I think back on this today, I realize that these night shift attendants did not have any proper training to help them deal with the patients. Most of them hadn't even taken a nurse's aid course. I found out that the hospital didn't even do background checks on these people.

I am not trying to point a finger at anyone in particular although I certainly could! I just want the public to be aware and to find out as much as possible about the qualifications of caregivers. This is critical if you have someone housed in any facility where they depend on the staff for their basic needs.

As sure as I am sitting here writing this book, I am telling you that some people who are hired to work in our hospitals and nursing homes (which are so terribly understaffed) have severe emotional problems themselves and should never be dealing with the public. They have no idea how truly sick some of the patients are. The care some patients are given does nothing but further kill their spirits and sometimes worse.

Chapter Eleven

On a lighter note, I loved to play softball. At Boston State Hospital, I got some of the student nurses and the female attendants together, and we would play. I wish I had my video camera then because they were so very funny. Some of them didn't know how to hold a bat, never mind catch a ball. I tried so hard to teach them, and it felt good when they finally learned. I believe they had great fun when they finally got the hang of it. I thank you, girls, for giving it your all. As slight as it may seem, those were the times I felt good about myself.

As I write about this time at the hospital, there is one memory that will always haunt me. I was sixteen years old and had cut my leg in three places. It was early in the morning, and the staff had to wake up the doctor who was on call that night. He walked into the treatment room where I was sitting with the head nurse. This was a procedure I had gone through each and every time I hurt myself, and by then, I didn't care if the doctor showed up or not. He mumbled that he had just gotten to sleep when the call came in about me. He told me to get up on the table, and through squinty eyes, he checked my leg. The way he said that I was the reason he had to get up really scared me, but I didn't say anything. The doctor said, "It's going to take two shots of Novocain to numb each cut and two sutures to close each one, so I am not going to bother to numb the area. Maybe you will learn a lesson from this and think twice before you cut yourself again."

With that, the nurse put her arm across my stomach, with her back to me and not a word said. When he started to suture my cuts, I grabbed on to the back of the nurse's sweater and just hung on. By the time he was finished stitching all three cuts, her sweater was in a tight ball from my sweaty hand where I had been hanging on, but I never gave him the satisfaction of seeing me cry. I held back the tears, slid my body off the table, and left the room. I walked back to my room where I sat on the window ledge and finally started to cry. How could he do that to me, the nurse holding me down and neither one of them saying a word of comfort? It was bad enough that I had hurt myself, but he had hurt me too.

I was so distraught and angry about the incident that I grabbed a common pin and a piece of glass and removed every one of the stitches, put them in a napkin, and walked down to the office where the head nurse was sitting. I laid the napkin in front of her and said, "Tell the doctor for me that there was no lesson learned!" With all of my heart, I hope that man is not practicing medicine today.

So many things went on in those state hospitals that were just wrong. I saw quite a bit, but being so young, I had no voice. I kept it all to myself.

During the time spent there, I met a few girls who were abusing themselves. I remember one girl in particular. We were good friends, and she would swallow anything she could fit into her mouth. Most of the time, she took pills that she had saved up and gotten from other patients. It seemed that she was always being taken to the medical building to have her stomach pumped. One night, I awoke to see the night crew rushing around trying to wake her up. An ambulance finally came and took her out. I kept asking how she was but was told to go back to bed. I lay there all night thinking and hoping that she would be okay. When the morning shift came, I asked them to please call the medical building to see if she was still there and if anyone knew how she was doing. I was told that they would let me know when they got any information. Hours and hours went by, and I went to the nurses and asked again about my friend. That is when they finally told me that she had died. I missed her so much. I think people thought that just because we self-injured, we have no feelings. That was not the case; we just didn't know how to deal with our feelings.

Some of my hospital stays are vague and others quite vivid. I have pushed so much down over the years, trying to forget what happened to me. When I was allowed to come home from the hospital on weekends, my poor mother would tell me to put a long-sleeved blouse on so no one could see my arms. Oh, how ashamed she must have felt about what I was doing to myself. If only we could have communicated; somehow I might have felt a little better about myself. She didn't know just how much I hated myself—how I felt so ugly, dirty, and out of place. I didn't seem to fit in anywhere. The only places I truly seemed to fit in were in the hospitals where there were other girls my age suffering with self-abuse issues. Their reasons for the self-abuse may have been slightly different, but somehow we all seemed very much the same.

One day at the Massachusetts Mental Health Center, my mom came to visit. I had no idea she was coming. About two hours before her arrival, I had put my hand through a window, again requiring more sutures and, of course, the seclusion room. When my mother arrived, the nurse opened the door and came in to let me know, but she said I would not be allowed to visit with her. When I asked why, she replied that she felt I was not calm enough. I pleaded with her to let me visit with my mom, but she refused. With that, I called her a bitch. I hadn't realized that the door was still slightly open, and that my mother could hear me. My mother would never tolerate the vulgarity and disrespect I had shown this nurse, so she came right into the seclusion room and slapped me across the face. We did not swear in my family, at least not in front of my mother.

I truly felt that the nurse was wrong. Mom had come a very long way to reach the hospital, taking two separate buses as she didn't drive; and my father was working and not able to bring her. I loved my mom, and I hated the fact that this nurse wouldn't find it in her heart to at least let me see my mom even for five minutes. So I sat in the room and cried. I tore off the bandages and the cuts started bleeding again. I stood up in the middle of the room and splattered my blood on all four walls. Needless to say, when they finally let me out of the room, the nurse made me get a pail of hot water and wash the walls. No matter what I did, I just made it harder on myself.

That particular nurse was not very well liked by anyone at the hospital. She had a very stern face, never smiled or laughed, and acted like she was mad at the world. That particular scene had been a power trip for her. The staff generally understood that if you hurt yourself and were put in the seclusion room for a couple of hours, you were calm and were allowed to come out at that point. But sometimes, they abused the seclusion rooms. They did use them as a form of punishment and sometimes carried this to extremes.

The seclusion rooms were very small and always extremely hot, even in the summer with air-conditioning because no one had access to the thermostat. There was never anything in the room except the hard black rubber mattress; there were bars on the window and, behind the bars, frosted glass with the faint black shape of chicken wire. Walls of cinder blocks were painted a dull gray, which was depressing in itself. There was a small five-by-seven-inch window in the door, also with chicken wire so patients could be observed. Some patients were stripped of their clothing, and others were given a heavy dress to put on.

Sometimes there was a tub filled with warm water though sometimes cold water was used. I remember the tubs were quite large and stood on a one-footed wooden pedestal. After struggling with a nurse and several male attendants, a patient was put into the tub, and a canvas cover (which covered the entire top of the tub) was snapped in place. There was only a small hole in the canvas where the patient's head would stick out. Some of the patients were very claustrophobic and almost in a state of shock. The nurse would have to remain in the room as long as the patient was kept in the tub. She would sit in a chair and read a book, never realizing the horrid and frightful feelings that these patients were experiencing at the time. The nurse, however, was just following the doctor's orders, assuming the patient would calm down in about a half hour or so.

Some patients, while sitting in the day hall, would use their fingernails to scratch at their faces and arms until they bled. Some would bite themselves and pull at their hair. Restraints were used frequently. The patients' hands and feet would be tied to their beds and would stay that way until they wore themselves out. Again, at times, the drug Thorazine was used. Many of the patients were left in a somewhat catatonic state from receiving high doses of the drug. They were so bad that they couldn't speak. Patients were given a series of electric shock treatments to try to "bring them back to reality." It helped some, or so I would like to believe, but the majority did not benefit from this type of treatment. In fact, this procedure left some of them worse off than before. Some of these poor souls are still locked up in the back wards of these hospitals today.

While at home late one night, I cut the main artery in my wrist and ended up at Boston City Hospital. They had to come into my room and changed the bandages several times during the night. At about three in the morning, a nurse came in with a roll of bandages and scissors. She laid them both on the nightstand beside my bed and took my hand in hers. She started to remove the bloody bandage from my wrist, and as she reached for the scissors, I also reached for them. She grabbed for my good wrist and pried the scissors out of my hand without saying a word. Once again, she started to remove the bloody bandage; and again, I grabbed the scissors as she put them down. This scenario was repeated several times until one time, she was unable to wrestle the scissors from my hand as I rolled over on my side and held them close to me. She held on to my hand and me until the sun rose hours later. Neither of us slept. That nurse knew exactly what she was doing and had read me like a book. I know for a fact that she could have gotten those scissors away from me if she had really tried. I really just wanted someone to stay with me that night. The feeling that I recall was of safety, comfort, and warmth. Thank you!

My self-injury lasted for about eight or nine years. Aren't those supposed to be the best years of a child's life? That is something I will never know!

Chapter Twelve

I loved my mom, and I would have given anything for us to be closer. As she got older, I was the only one who reached out my arms to hold her. It is so very sad that we lost out on so many years. But there comes a time when we have to let go of the past in order to have a future. We may still go back in our minds from time to time and remember things that have happened to us that were unpleasant, but we must move forward and let go of the guilt and anger.

I was well into my thirties, and the hospitals were far behind me. I remember so well when I went into the Painters' Union where my older brother, Jackie, was a mason. We both worked on one of the dorms at Harvard University. Sad to say, my brother had a very bad drinking problem. He would work all morning, and at lunch, he would head to the nearest bar to drink. I was visiting my mother one Saturday; my brother lived with her. He came in after working overtime on a job, grabbed a beer, and sat down at the one end of the couch with my mother at the other end. My brother took out his paycheck and showed it to my mom. She said how great it was, and then he read the amount to me. It was quite a large sum. When I mentioned how much I made (which was more than his, minus the overtime), Mom told me not to boast. I felt so bad. She had no idea how hard I worked. I think I was just looking for her to say that she thought my check was great also and to give me a little encouragement.

I realize now that my mother could not change her ways. I broke through a lot of barriers in her mind. I came into this world too soon; I was a nineties woman in the sixties. I believe that in my mother's heart, she wished she could have done half the things I did. I am a free-spirited person and will always be so. I have no regrets, except for the obvious—my self-abuse. Having done those things to myself is something I will always regret and have to live with. It is still hard at times when I meet new people; I still tend to wear long sleeves even when it is very hot out. One day, I hope to stop feeling ashamed of my scars. If I were to find a bottle with a genie in it, and she said I could have three wishes, the first would be to see what my body would look like without all the scars. Second, I would wish that everyone who does so would stop abusing themselves; and of course, the third and final wish would be for three more wishes (I am not totally crazy!).

It was in my late teens when I met the man I was going to marry. He was a quiet man with a drinking problem. He was a gentle man who was very patient with me and never forced himself on me the way others had. He knew about my self-abuse and stood by me all the way. I remember asking him several times how he could love me, knowing what I did to myself, and he said, "I just do and will always love you, no matter what." When I think back, he did stand by me and love me, but I didn't love myself, so how could I give love to him the way he deserved it? I loved him in my own way, but self-abuse came first, and that was a big part of my life.

One night, I was drinking whiskey and headed for an abandoned hallway, alone as usual. Earlier that night, I had purchased a box of razor blades and had them in my pocket. Sometimes when I did this, I would not use them; but for some reason, I always had to have them with me. I slipped off my long winter coat and decided to cut my back. By this time, the bottle of whiskey was half-gone. I was feeling pretty bad and lonely as usual. I reached my arm up under my blouse and sweater and pulled the razor from the middle down to the lower part of my back. I felt no pain. I cut more and deeper. When I finally stopped, all I could feel was the warm blood running down my back and stopping at the waistband of my wool slacks. I sat there for a while until the other half of the whiskey was gone. I pulled my blouse and sweater close to my back to stop the bleeding, put my coat back on, buttoned it up, and headed back to the Spa.

As I sat at the Spa across from my friend Joanne, I felt the blood still trickling down my back. We sat there talking and laughing until I finally told her what I had done to myself. It was no surprise to her because she knew I used to cut myself. She got up from her side of the table and pushed in beside me and asked to see my back. I dropped my coat to my waist. She quickly took a look and told me the cuts were very deep and that I should go to the hospital. By then, I was starting to feel sick. All I wanted to do was to go home and to lie down in my bedroom. I told her I would go the hospital, and I left.

I went home, and all I can remember is waking up in the morning with my blouse still on and stuck to my back with the dried blood. I got up, went into the bathroom, filled the tub with warm water, and slowly lowered my stiffened body into the water. As I soaked, the water turned light pink all around me. Then I realized just how deeply I must have cut myself. Finally,

I worked my blouse away from my back. My back was still seeping blood. I disposed of my blouse so my mother would not find it and went back into my room and turned my back to the mirror. When I saw the blood still trickling down my back, I decided to call the doctor at Boston City Hospital. She was one of my doctors when I was a patient at the state hospital. She was basically the only one I trusted. I told her what I had done the night before and how deep the cuts were. She told me to come into the emergency room right away and to ask for her. She said that she would be there all day and into the night.

For some reason, I didn't end up going to the emergency room until early evening. I just could not leave my room that day. The doctor came down to see me. She closed the curtain around us and started to clean my back with a warm solution of antibiotics and water. She told me the cuts were very deep but could not be stitched. She closed and bandaged them the best she could and took me upstairs to her office where we talked for quite a while. She suggested I return to Boston State Hospital.

My Wedding, 1964

I did go back to Boston State for some time; and my boyfriend, who later became my husband, would come to visit me at the hospital. Sometimes he would come with my mother. At twenty-one, I got married and, a year later, had my son, James. Let me tell you, when they placed that little bundle of seven pounds and four ounces of love into my arms, I just looked down at him and cried. I finally knew what love meant. That was when my life started to change. Slowly, as my son grew, so did I. I cannot say that having my son was the cure for me, but he played a big part in my wanting to change.

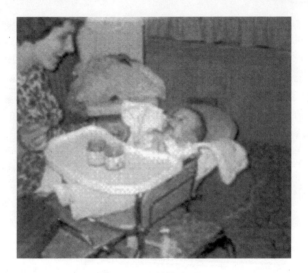

Myself and Jimmy

My marriage eventually ended in separation, and I became a single parent. During that time, I was hospitalized once briefly; but as time passed and my son got older, the self-injury stopped. In my struggle to protect my son, I underwent a series of painful dermabrasion procedures to try to disguise my scars as burns. They would be easier for me to explain to him and to his friends. I was effectively burying the scars even deeper.

As I took the final steps leaving the hospital, I was going back into society and the so-called real world knowing in my heart that no matter what, sink or swim, I was never going back. I would never again be locked in a room having to beg for a glass of water and waiting hours for someone to come and unlock the door so I could use the bathroom. I would die before I ever let that happen to me again. Things were going to be up to me from there on!

Chapter Thirteen

Sometimes it only takes one person to make you feel good about yourself, and you suddenly look inside and really think about who and what you are. Only then can you begin to change. I used to be referred to as fidgety because I had such a hard time sitting still; I was always on the go but usually in the wrong direction. But when I had my son, I found direction and learned a great deal; through him, I found myself. I tried to show him the right way and how to be confident in whatever he did.

James's love of music started when he was about seven years old. We were out shopping, and we walked by a music store. He stopped to look at a guitar in a store window, his eyes as big as saucers. I asked him if he would like to play, and we went inside to ask the price. It was fifty dollars, which to me back then was a great deal of money, but I could see that this really meant something to Jim. I had a good feeling about this guitar and my son, so I found the means to purchase it for him.

I started asking around and found out that my mailman played in a band, and I also asked if he would give Jim lessons when he finished his route. He agreed to come by once each week for two dollars. Jim was so excited. Then one day, the mailman brought Jim to me and said we all had to talk. He told me that he could tell that Jim was not practicing and that he should if I was paying good money for his lessons and he was taking the time to teach him. I turned to Jim and said, "Make up your mind right now. You can stop taking lessons and keep the guitar to just fool around with, or you can keep taking lessons, but I am not going to be calling you into the house to practice. This is your responsibility, not mine."

Right there and then, Jim said, "I want to play real good someday. I promise I will practice."

From then on, he'd come home from school and go straight to his room and practice. His teacher noticed the change right away and said that Jim was doing really well. Jim would call me up to his room at night to show me what he had learned. I would lie on his top bunk and listen to him play; and no matter how bad he sounded, I would always say, "That's great, Jim. Now play it again." I can remember passing by his room in the evening and looking in to see him sitting there—still in his school pants, T-shirt, and the sweat rolling down his cheeks—as he practiced over and over again to get it just right. As I look back, I think that he must have been lonely as an only child facing life with his parents separated.

Jimmy, 1972

Time went by so quickly that soon Jim was in junior high school and putting a band together. His cousins lived close by and one of them played drums and another was taking bass guitar lessons, so they spent a great deal of time together. Music became Jim's big dream.

Jim, 1985

Chapter Fourteen

I have spoken over the years with my sisters, Mary and Jane, about how they remember the younger days. When I was about seven, before my self-abuse started, I had my tonsils out. Mary took all of her babysitting money and bought what looked like the whole store for me. She sat on the couch and had me sit on a big overstuffed chair, and she reached behind the couch and presented me with one gift after another. I don't recall how many gifts there were, but I do remember the gift of love and happiness on both of our faces. She was so happy giving to me, and I was delighted with all of the special attention.

Mary and I sometimes reminisce about how we loved playing house together. She was always dressed up in Mom's dresses, and I would wear my father's long white dress shirt. Mary always made the rules; I was to be her boyfriend, and she was a singer in a nightclub. I had to pretend to pick her up at her house and walk her to the club. We would walk through the house about six or seven times before we felt that we had reached the club (which was the bathroom). She'd then stand up on the toilet seat and pretend that she was on stage while I sat on the edge of the tub. Back in those days, tubs were very small with extremely narrow edges (need I say more?). I sat there loving every moment of it, and she did her whole act. After every song, I would clap loudly and we would imagine that the club was packed with people, all of whom thought that Mary was a great singer. Then Mary would have me go out and change clothes and come back in as a different boyfriend. I'd have to enter the bathroom-club very slowly as if it was packed with people. She would wave to me from her toilet-seat stage like she was having a hard time seeing me though the crowd. Yes, Mary, you were and still are great! How wonderful it was for you to let me get lost in your imagination.

We all thought that Mary would become a schoolteacher at one time because she loved to gather up the neighborhood kids and set up our back hallway like a classroom. We'd all sit on the stairs with two kids on each step. I always got to sit on the bottom step closest to Mary, and some of the other kids complained to Mary about this. She just said, "She can sit there. She's my sister, and I'm the teacher!" No one would ever argue with Mary. I personally think Mary would have made a wonderful nun, but I don't think there is a nun out there who is half the angel Mary is.

The more Mary and I talked as adults, the more she remembered the sorrow she felt when she saw me suffering with earaches. Mom used to put hot oil in my ear, and I would have to stay in bed, lying on the hot water bottle for what seemed like hours. It hurt so much that I cried. We also discussed the time I got scratched by the family cat. It became so infected that I had to be operated on and spent about ten days in the hospital. When I got home, I had to soak my arm three times a day, and it was extremely painful. I missed a great deal of school.

We loved to play "grocery store" in the backyard. We would gather up stones, some big and some small, and use them as money. We found empty cans and cereal boxes and stacked them on the back porch. Marbles were also a big thing back then. There were two ways of playing: One was to draw a circle in the dirt and each player would put the same number of marbles inside the circle. Then each player would throw the bigger marble (called a shooter). The object of the game was to knock out as many marbles as possible from within circle. If one missed hitting a marble in the circle, it was the next person's turn. The other marble game was called Bunny Hole. We'd put the heel of our shoe in the dirt and spin around until the depth was just right for a bunny hole. Then we'd would draw a starting line with a stick and toss the marbles. The object was to get the marbles into the bunny hole. We loved this game, and all of our backyards got to look like they were overrun by rabbits.

My sister Mary (1953)

My sister Jane (1951)

My Mom (1951)

The most dangerous thing we delighted in doing was "hopping cars." It was not a smart thing to do, but back then, it just seemed like harmless fun. It was a winter game requiring snow. We'd stand on the street corner, crouching down behind a parked car, and wait for a car to come up the street. When it started to pass, we'd run up behind it and grab on to the bumper. Back then, bumpers were really big and easy to hold on to. We would slide along behind the car for as long as possible; it felt like skiing. Most drivers knew what we were doing and were pretty good about driving slowly. Then, of course, we would get a driver who would roll down his window and yell, "Hey, you kids, get the hell off my bumper!" Some of them would even stop their cars and chase us down the street, but that never stopped us from trying it again.

At this time, we lived on the second floor of a three-family house, so we would take turns keeping watch for the cars. One of us would sit down on the front porch, and as soon as we saw the headlights of a car at the end of our street, we would ring the doorbell for the one upstairs. She would grab her coat and gloves and rush down the stairs. The two of us would jump on each other and laugh all the way down the street. Then we'd let go and walk back to our house and wait for the next car. Now when we talk about this, we think how crazy we were, but we both agree that it was the most fun we ever had. Too bad we couldn't stay kids a little longer!

The three-family tenement houses that surrounded the whole neighborhood were all in a row, and across the street, they were lined up the same way. At the very top of the street, there was a cement circle where Jane taught me to ride a bike. That circle was a safe haven for all of the children in the neighborhood because that is where we could play all kinds of games like tin can relieve-o or hide-and-go-seek, or we could just sit as you see us in the picture below.

Jane on my left and Mary on my right.

This picture was taken when the three of us decided to go back and see the old neighborhood. Somehow I felt safe with my two sisters with me as we talked about some of the good times we had growing up.

I remember the time I talked the little boy across the street out of his cowboy pants, and left him in the hallway in his underwear. We were the same age, about seven, and all I wanted was to wear his cowboy pants. They were black with silver snaps and white fringes running down each leg. I was so fascinated with those pants, I just had to put them on no matter what. I loved them. I could care less about what he had in his underwear.

When Mary started dating and her dates picked her up at the house, I would stand at the window and watch them drive away, feeling so sad; it was as if I was losing her. She was always popular with the boys and had lots of friends. She could make anyone laugh, even at their lowest point. Mary, I am proud to call you my big sister, and I deeply apologize for the pain you had to endure while I was defacing my body all of those years.

Our games were a little harder for my sister Jane to remember because she was the oldest of the three and, being very much a lady, never did the things Mary and I would do. Jane was a loner, spending her time playing with paper dolls and her favorite doll, Peggy. I remember Jane always kept that doll looking great. Jane was good in school, and so my mom asked her to help me with my catechism to help prepare me for my first communion. My own mother had missed a great deal of schooling herself, so this job was passed on to Jane. She would go over the book with me and then ask me questions. I just could not come up with the answers, so she would instruct me to read it back to her. I had such a hard time making out the words; no one knew then that I had dyslexia. Jane would get angry with me because she felt that I just wasn't trying. As we talk now, there is a pained look on her face because she cannot remember those times, and they are so clear to me. She did remember, as we got older, asking me to go shopping and to the dentist with her. I always agreed to go, and that made her dentist appointment not seem quite as bad. She also remembered when we got holes in our shoes; and Dad would measure our feet, cut out a piece of cardboard from a cereal box, and stick it into the shoe.

When Jane met her husband, Joe, she was fourteen. They got married when Jane turned eighteen and are, to this day, a devoted couple. They have brought eight beautiful children into this world. And when you ask Jane what their secret of a long and lasting marriage is, she replies, "He is my best friend." It is very obvious when you see Jane and Joe together.

We sometimes talk about my softball team and that one particular Saturday afternoon when I had practice. Mary and Jane were both married by then, and Mary was expecting her first baby. Jane was visiting Mary, and I told them I would be back right after practice. Mary's house was not far from the softball field. Well, one of the girls on my team was giving me a hard time, so I left early. It bothered me terribly because I loved softball and was always the last to leave. When I got to Mary's house, I started to cry, and they both asked me what had happened. I told them that the huge blister I had on my batting hand had been really painful every time I swung the bat, but I kept trying. This one girl kept making nasty remarks to me like, "You stink, Connie, go home. You can't hit the ball for beans."

It hurt both my hand and my feelings, so I left. Well, Mary was the one who always stuck up for me; but this time, Jane got very mad and asked if the team was still at the field. When I told her yes, she said, "Let's go!" Mary was in her last month of her pregnancy, so she stayed home and sat this one out.

When we got to the field, Jane called to the girl over and really told her off. She said, "Where do you get off treating my sister like that or, for that matter, any teammate?" Then, when she'd finished scolding her soundly, she turned to me and said, "Let's go!" I don't know what came over me, but I got very upset and turned and punched the girl right in the mouth. She went down, and her mouth started to bleed. I was a little scared, but I was glad that I'd hit her. Jane panicked. She grabbed my arm and pulled me away, practically dragging me home.

Mary wanted to know exactly what had happened, and I said, "Mary, you would have been so proud of me. I finally stuck up for myself."

All Mary could say was, "Oh crap, I wish I'd been there to see you in action." Jane was really upset and asked if we were both crazy. She couldn't understand why I had hit the girl and then scolded me for doing so. Mary just looked at me and winked, letting me know that she understood how I felt and why I reacted that way. But that time, Jane too was there for me when it really mattered.

The next day, I was sent to see the priest for what I'd done. The first thing he said to me was that no matter what, you never ever hit your teammate. He told me that he was left with no choice in the matter; I was being taken off the team. He didn't even listen to me when I tried to tell him what had happened. I agreed that I was wrong in hitting someone but couldn't understand why I was the only one being punished. She was still allowed to play on the team, and I wasn't!

The more Jane and I talk now, the more she remembers things about growing up. We had this game where Jane would lie on her back on the couch or bed and take hold of Mary's hands, and then putting her feet against Mary's stomach, she would hoist her up against the wall. She would then let go of Mary's hands, and Mary would move her arms and feet back and forth like a fish in water. Jane called the game Fish on the Wall. I loved when it was my turn and would plead with them to keep playing. It seemed that we played for hours this way.

One night, we were playing Fish on the Wall in the bedroom; and I was up on the wall when, all of a sudden, Mary yelled, "Get down! Here comes Mom!" Jane tried to get me down so fast that I slipped off her feet and slammed my fanny into the bottom drawer of the dresser. For a very long time, we could not get that drawer open; and boy, was my fanny sore.

We talked about the time all three of us worked at the A&W Root Beer. It was one of those drive-up restaurants where the carhops would come to your car to take your order. They only served hamburgers and root beer. They had funny names for the hamburgers like Papa-Burger, Momma-Burger, and Baby-Burger. The Baby-Burger was my favorite. Jane was always on time for work, but Mary and I were almost always late. Every time I got to work, the boss would hand me a Baby-Burger and tell me to hurry up and get the hell out to take care of the customers. He was a very nice guy and always said it with a chuckle. He knew we were really good workers.

Jane told me that she didn't understand how I could hurt myself the way I did. I wish I could make them understand how very sorry I am for hurting my whole family that way. When you have those awful feelings, you don't take the time to stop and think about anything else; you just act on the feelings. Both Mary and Jane said that they felt mad every time they saw my arms all bandaged up, and they felt that I was doing it to get attention. That was partly true, but the other side is that I really didn't like myself; I honestly hated myself then. When I think of it today, I am struck by the idea that it was far too high price to pay to gain attention and self-worth!

We always thought of Jane as the matriarch of the family. She felt that she had to be the strong one and set a good example. Jane is a very smart woman and thinks things through in a logical way. I don't think that she has been told often enough what a beautiful person she really is. Jane, you are not only smart but caring, giving, and thoughtful. As I have grown older, I realize that no matter what has taken place in my life, you have always been there for me—always offering a shoulder to cry on, your friendship (which means so much to me), and your home to come to. You will never truly realize how good you have made me feel. Thank you, Jane, from the bottom of my heart.

As an adult, when I traveled back to Boston to visit, I'd watch Jane with our mom, and as little as it seemed to Jane, what she did for Mom was so appreciated. She would bring her dinner, having made extra for her own family so that she would have some to bring to Mom. Jane, you always had something in your hands for Mom when you came through her door, whether it was food or something you picked up for her while shopping.

Jane's life was very regimented, and she always did things on certain days. I guess that is what you have to do when you are raising eight children and taking care of a husband. When her husband came home from work each day, the entire family would sit down to eat together. They attended church as a family and took day trips to the park as a family as well. They were together no matter what. Jane made sure of that.

Joe worked for a large advertising company as an electrician and never missed a day of work. Jane still found time to work part-time in a coupon business. She would cut out all the coupons she could get her hands on, and what she couldn't use, she mailed to other members of her group. While Joe slept, Jane stayed up late, cutting out coupons and answering all the mail she received from others doing the same. She was so good at organizing this whole thing that when we all went shopping together, it was standard fair for Jane to have double and triple coupons for everything she wanted to purchase. Mary and I used to drive her crazy on those shopping days. Every time Jane would park her cart to go for something else in the store, Mary and I would find some ridiculous item that Jane didn't need (such as a fifty-pound bag of dog food) and stick it into her cart. We always ended up laughing our way through the shopping day.

When we all finally got ready to go through the checkout at the store, Mary had very few groceries, and I even less, but Jane's cart was overflowing. Her bill would average about one hundred dollars, but once the checkout girl added in all of Jane's coupons, she hadn't spent more than about twenty-five dollars. Even in the 1960s, that was very little for the quantity she had purchased.

Jane, Mary and Connie

Mary is another very strong character; she hides her tears with laughter. You cannot have a conversation with Mary without ending up laughing. Even when her eyes are filled with pain, somehow they become tears of laughter. That is the thing that Mary does best. I never had to go to the Comedy Connection while I was growing up; I grew up with the best comedian I'll ever know.

Mary and I laugh so hard about the time she found a button while she was out in the school yard for recess. We were in grade school. When she got back to her classroom, she asked her teacher if she cold go around to the other classrooms to see who might have lost a button. The teacher said yes, and off she went. Well, I was about seven at the time and was sitting in my class when in came Mary with this button and said to my teacher, "Ms. Kelly, I found this button. May I see if anyone in your class lost it?"

Ms. Kelly said, "Yes, you may go up and down the aisle and let everyone see it." Of course, when Mary got to me, she said something funny, and I cracked up with laughter. Ms. Kelly spoke right up and said, "Are you done, Mary? You may go now."

"Thank you, Ms. Kelly," replied Mary very politely; and of course, when she got out in the hall where Ms. Kelly couldn't see her, she started to dance and make funny faces back at me, and the whole class laughed. Then she was gone in a flash.

About three weeks went by, and in came Mary again with another button; this one, she had removed from the bottom of her own blouse, the part that you tuck in so no one sees it anyway. Mary didn't even finish her sentence when Ms. Kelly said, "Mary, just hold the button up in front of the class." Again, when Mary left the room, she just had to turn and do something funny to crack me up. With that, Ms. Kelly got up and closed the door. And Mary went on to the next room. Mary loved getting out of her class any way she could.

Mom always gave us are own milk money. On the way to school, Mary would ask me for my milk money and said she would tell her teacher just before lunch that she had to go and give me my money for milk. Now some fifty years later, she is still cracking me up with that wonderful, funny personality of hers.

And then there is me—the Hugger. My family didn't hug one another; and after all of those years, I realize how comforting hugs really are, and God knows they were long overdue. I was not the only one who needed the closeness; it was my whole family. Now at least I can say that I had the chance to teach my mom that the human heart needs touch and hugs. In the last year of Mom's life when I was home with her, I always bent down to kiss her good night when I put her to bed. I would kiss her on the cheek several times, and when I looked at her eyes, they were all squinted with laughter. She would take my face in her hands and say, "Oh, you, Connie! God love you and keep you safe this night." Then she would kiss me back, and I could feel the strength in her little hands as if she was saying, "Here is all the love and attention I was not able to give you when you were younger, but at least we have it now."

Chapter Fifteen

Being the youngest of five, feeling so lost and empty, I never seemed to fit in anywhere. It seemed I was always looking in at the world from the outside—always hungry, not for food but for love and attention. I was always cold, not from the lack of clothes but for the warmth of a hand holding mine.

Let me tell you about one of the few safe and warm memories I do have. When you read this, I hope it warms your heart as much as it warms mine as I write it.

It was the week before Christmas when my dad would stop on his way home from work and pick up the Christmas tree. While lying in my bed, I would hear him and Mom talking about how nice and full the tree looked as he'd shake the light snow that had accumulated on the branches during his long journey home. He'd stand the tree up against the living room wall and say he would build a stand for it in the morning. I remember staring out at the tree from my bedroom, and even though it was not yet decorated, it always looked beautiful to me. As the streetlight shone through the window and reflected the empty branches up on the ceiling and against the wall, it took on the look of a beautiful big butterfly. Finally, I would fall asleep.

The next day, I could not wait to get up and watch my dad fiddle around with all his tools, trying to make the best stand he could. As I remember, he always had to saw off the bottom of the tree so it would not hit the ceiling. The stand always had two pieces of wood, which ended up looking like a crucifix. The aroma of pine would fill the room as it slowly seeped from the butt of the stem. It always gave the feeling that Christmas was right around the corner. Then Dad would go off to work and leave the decorating to Mom and us children.

I was always in hurry. I didn't care where I put anything as long as it got done. My favorite time was at night when I could lie on the floor with my head under the tree and look up at all the shimmering lights. Mom would take pains with getting it just right, small bulbs at the top, big bulbs at the bottom, not to mention the tinsel that had to be put on one strand at a time. It all seemed to take forever. I remember times when Mom was not looking, I would go around the back of the tree, take a handful of tinsel, and toss it on the branches, saying, "All done back here!" If I left the room for any reason, when I returned, my clump of tinsel would be straightened out.

Well, finally, the tree was done. As a light snow gathered on the sill and the cold from outside left little mounds of frost along the window—which always looked like mountains to me—in the window, one single candlestick with a white light shinning brightly always completed the picture. My most favorite time of all was when night fell. When it was time to get ready for bed, I could not wait to slip my cold legs into my warmed pajamas that Mom would lay across the big door of the old black kitchen stove. I would head right for the Christmas tree, wiggle my way under it, and just lie there for hours. I think back to that tender age and remember how safe and happy I felt under that Christmas tree.

My two brothers were much older than us girls. But I do have some good memories of being with them.

I remember asking my mom if one of my camp counselors could come for lunch one Sunday, and Mom went out of her way to make it special.

My brother Jim worked on weekends, so he would get up late. While I was sitting having lunch with my counselor, Jim came into the kitchen, opened the fridge, and took out the orange juice pitcher. He then proceeded to pour a glass of juice, precisely the way my mother would.

Mom always filled the glass halfway and then poured it back into the pitcher. She would do this three of four times to mix the juice. Jim started mixing the juice, standing at the table in his pants and a T-shirt, not saying a word.

My counselor asked, "Why are you doing that?"

Jim replied, "I can't make up my mind," and smiled and walked away. I was mortified that he could not have been a little nicer to my guest and at least say hello. I was about twelve years old, and all I know was I wanted that day to be very special. I did not realize back then that I had a huge crush on this girl. As much as that hurt my feelings back then, of course, when I think of it today, Jim was just trying to be funny; and I laugh now when I think about it.

Brother Jim went into the navy. I was about thirteen years old; I remember getting a few letters from him. One year, he sent me a beautiful necklace with matching earrings and bracelet. I still have them after all these years.

When I was a patient at Mass Mental Health Center, I used to go upstairs where they had a pool table, and one of the nicer male attendants taught me how to shoot. I was very good with my hands, and I picked it up very easily. Stuff like that came easy for me.

Brother Jim was home on leave and came to visit me at the hospital one day, and of course, I was not on the ward but upstairs shooting pool, so they sent Jim up. Boy, did he look great in his navy whites; I was so proud and very glad to see him. Jim asked me if I could play pool. I said, "A little."

Jim replied, "Let's play a game." After the game, Jim smiled at me and said, "Where did you learn how to shoot like that? You're good, Connie!"

Later in life, I found out that when Jim was a young teenager and did not have money to take his girlfriend out to a movie, he would head for the pool room. The bigger guys would bet money that Jim could not beat them. Need I say more? Jim was unbeatable.

Growing up, I never saw much of my other brother, Jackie. He was much older then I was, and he was a long-distance truck driver. He was always on the road; at times, he would be gone for months. Jack was a quiet man, a lot like my dad. One Christmas, as a young child, I do remember Jackie coming home. I was in the living room, just sitting looking at the Christmas tree like I always did. He came over to me and put this little stuffed animal in my hands. I remember it was a lamb, curly and so soft, with a little pink nose. I loved it, but I don't remember Jackie ever talking to me that much when I was younger.

Chapter Sixteen

My mother was a woman who didn't have very much growing up because her family was very large and very poor. She was the oldest of twelve and had many chores on the family farm. She had to tend to the chickens, cows, and sheep. My mom used to tell me about her dog, Daisy, and how Daisy would help when it was time to bring the cows in for the night. Apparently, Daisy had some herding instincts because she would nip at the cows' legs to get them to move along toward the farm each night. What a help and joy that dog was to my mother. Mom loved that dog, and Daisy followed her everywhere. When it was time for supper, Daisy would find her place on the floor right beside my mom and would sometimes stick her nose into Mom's lap to ask for food. She made a point of sharing something of the little she had with her companion. Some nights, all they had to eat was a boiled potato and a glass of milk, but Mom always shared with Daisy.

Mom spent her days out in the fields picking potatoes; that was their livelihood. Her teachers would ask her to try to come to school more often because she was such a bright young girl and so willing to listen and learn. How sad to think that there was someone who loved going to school, but because her family depended on her working the fields, she couldn't follow her heart.

My mom continued supporting her family after she came to the United States while one of her sisters came to the States and went to college and married well and eventually traveled the world. It all seemed so unfair somehow; Mom may have done so many things differently in her life had she been given the opportunity to experience a real education.

Traveling back and forth to Boston once I had moved away, I did a lot of reminiscing. As I sat on my mother's couch early one morning, my head kept bobbing back and forth as I looked down the hall toward her bedroom. I couldn't wait to see her little head peeping out of her doorway. Her eyesight was very bad then, and she struggled to see who was sitting on her couch. Finally, as she walked slowly toward me, her eyes squinting to see, I came into focus. "Well, good morning, Connie," she said. "Did you sleep well?" Then she headed for the kitchen to make us tea and toast, the morning ritual.

I stood right up and gave her a big hug and kiss. I could feel her frail body in my arms. She was so small, I had to bend way down to hug her; and she hugged me very tightly, letting me know how much she loved me.

On every trip home to Boston to see my mom, I never left before cutting her toenails. It was amazing, but when I was working in the nursing homes, there were two things I disliked doing: the first was washing someone's false teeth, and the other was cutting toenails. But it was different with my mom. I would have her sit on her couch, and I tried to make her feel like a queen; I'd bring in a pan of warm soapy water, and I would wash her little legs and her feet. After cutting her nails, I would rub her legs and feet with lotion and then put her leg warmers and slippers on. After I was all done, she would always say to me, "Connie, you make me feel like a new woman."

It sure did not take much to make Mom happy. I guess that was my way of saying, "Thank you, Mom, for all the long trips you made to the hospitals in the rain and snow."

I stayed eleven days for that trip and had five hours to get back to Tennessee. My visit was a tough one because Mom had to be admitted to the hospital for three days while I was there. When Mary and I brought her back home, she was very unsteady on her feet and seemed so confused. I hated leaving but knew that she was in the best care with Mary at her side and Jane stopping over to help out regularly. I knew that I would be returning to Boston very soon.

When I got off the plane in Tennessee, I was totally stressed out, and my head was pounding between concern over Mom and the fact that I hate to fly. But as soon as I looked up and saw my son's smiling face, I felt content. He always hugged me freely. He was brought up with lots of hugs and kisses; it's second nature to him, and I hope he always shows his affection that way.

When I arrived back at my apartment, I called Boston to see how Mom was doing. She had taken a bad fall just before I left and had gashed her leg terribly. Her poor little legs had gotten so frail and her skin so thin that she bled and bruised easily. Mary and I had taken it nice and slow with her, putting a pillow under her head and talking with her for a while before we got her back up. We were afraid she would fall again.

Before I moved to Tennessee, I was in Massachusetts, running a one-hour photo and custom-framing shop. I had taken my life's savings and opened the business. I thought it was something I could make a good living doing. Well, it turned out to be a very expensive business to run; chemistry and paper were costly, and I was situated in a small strip mall, so there was not a lot of foot traffic. If I had just stayed with the custom-framing side of the business, I believe I could have made it work.

It was rather scary opening the shop, but my son, Jim, worked right along with me. He even went to New Jersey and took a weeklong course on running the various machines needed for the processing. I had previously taken a photography course and worked in various photo labs, but this was certainly a completely new experience. I watched everything that Jim did so that I could learn as well.

Jim working at the shop

Jim was really great with people, even though he doesn't give himself enough credit. He waited on the customers with me, ran the machines and, at many times, opened the store for me in the morning so I could catch up on some much-needed rest.

I was living in a cottage in Lakeville, Massachusetts, during this time in my life. That in itself was a great deal to contend with as there was running water only six months of the year. When the water was turned off, I had to bring jugs of water from the shop to the cottage and heat the water on the stove to do dishes and wash. I also had a septic pump hooked up to the toilet.

I decided to join a local health club for the months I didn't have water. I would get up very early, go to the club, and shower there, then head to the shop. I lived like this for five years; and at times, it was so difficult, especially when it snowed. Believe me, the scenery was breathtaking as the cottage was in the woods, and everything looked beautiful; but having to worry about shoveling my car out of an unpaved driveway, head to the club to shower, and then get to the shop on time was almost too much for me.

In the summer months, the cottage was delightful. I could sit out and watch the squirrels and other wildlife. Many times, I would have my friends and family there for a cookout, and everyone just loved the peace and quiet of "Connie's little cottage" and said that it always had a calming effect on them.

My mom and sisters lived in the city with its hustle-bustle lifestyle. Mary worked for a school bus company that transported special needs children from one end of the city to the other. She would be up and out at five in the morning then back home to attend to Mom's needs. She needed time to unwind and relax and looked forward to coming to the cottage for visits.

Jane especially loved coming to the cottage. She had been dealing with her youngest daughter's battle with bulimia (and had been since Bonnie was thirteen) and needed to get away and talk things through with her family. It really appeared to help Jane; she could feel less alone in her silent vigil over Bonnie. Eventually, at the tender age of twenty-nine, Bonnie lost her battle to this terrible disease and it took its toll on all of us.

I can honestly say that those times we all spent at the cottage helped Jane get through some of the hardest years of her life. We all agreed that being together in this quiet setting was good, healthy therapy. We would laugh, cry, take long walks in the woods, and then go back to my place for my famous macaroni and cheese. Jane always brought the bread, and Mary brought the pastry. For these times, I loved my little cottage.

How wonderful it was to just sit back at the end of the day with a cup of tea and soak up the calm and beautiful smells emanating from the woods. It seemed to embrace the three of us every time.

Every couple of weeks, I would receive a phone call from Mary asking if it was time for therapy yet. Little did we know that we were actually helping one another for real. The advice and closeness was there for the taking and didn't cost a dime!

Many of my friends came down to Lakeville to spend a day or two. Somehow the evening never ended without someone bringing up their past experience with sexual abuse. I remember cringing each time the topic came up and squirming in my seat until the conversation moved on. I would feel the sweat running down my armpits, and the more they talked about the details, the more uncomfortable I'd become until I'd have to get up and slowly edge my way out into the front yard where I could drink in the warm night air and the smell of pine trees as I slowly composed myself. How sad I feel when I think back to that time, never realizing that these were the very things that were eating away at the core of my being.

Chapter Seventeen

The time came for Jim to move on, and he decided on Tennessee because of his musical aspirations. He had been shaping and molding his playing since age seven, going from country to blues and then swing. Jim felt that Nashville was where he might really be able to get a foothold on the music industry.

He seemed happiest when he played the blues, and I felt he would someday gravitate back to his great love. But whatever and wherever Jim played, he gave his all and still does.

Jim's father and I decided to have a going-away party for him. We rented a huge hall, and I told Jim that the get-together was for someone else, and we needed a band to play. At that time, Jim had a band of his own, so he agreed to do the gig. He had no idea it was to be his night. I was also able to get a couple of other bands, people I had met through Jim's playing. He walked into the room with his guitar in hand intending to play for a room full of strangers, but the expression on his face changed to confusion as he looked around and saw only people he knew. His grandmother, aunts, and friends were all there to wish him well. We all had a wonderful time, and I don't think Jim will ever forget that night.

When Jim left and I was alone to run the shop, it became increasingly hard to get everything done. I was working twelve-hour days six to seven days every week. I was totally beat but couldn't afford to hire any help. I did that for about one more year and then hired a friend of mine who was willing to work alongside with me for very little pay. She knew I could not afford much, but I did do some custom framing for her for free. It all worked out for a while, but the money was going out faster than it was coming in.

Before I opened my own business, I worked part-time at a one-hour photo and custom-frame shop. Back then, I had time on my hands and felt I had to do something more. One morning, I picked up the newspaper and found an ad looking for someone to teach line dancing at the Senior Citizens' Hall. I knew it would be great not only for the seniors but for myself as well because it would give me a chance to work with the elderly once again. I'd taken line dancing lessons when Jim was with a country-western band; he'd played at clubs all over Massachusetts, so I got a lot of practice. I loved every minute of it then and felt that it gave me the chance to express myself. It really brought the dancer out in me.

I decided to answer the ad. Working with the elderly is so rewarding; they open their hearts to you and never seem judgmental. That was where I needed to be at that point in my life. I got the job and started right away. Everyone who took the class was so intent on learning the dances. They were so cute, and I loved the class and all the new friends I made while I was there.

About the fourth class I instructed, a woman came through the door who I had never seen before. She had the biggest smile on her face and was joking with everyone in the place. It seemed that she had just gotten back from visiting her daughter in Virginia, and oh, could she dance. I could only think to myself, *There is no way this woman could be considered elderly*. She came to every class, and we became very good friends. Her name was Naomi, and she was fascinating to talk with.

One day, Naomi didn't show up for class. I asked the others if they knew if she was all right. One woman said, "She has something wrong with one of her eyes." When she didn't show up for the next two classes, I took it upon myself to give her a call. She asked if I would come visit her at her home, and I agreed. That was the beginning of the reconnection with my youth.

Naomi and her husband, Jim, would have me over; and we would sit for hours, relaxing on their screened porch, with ice tea or lemonade. The best thing was the wonderful conversations we three would share. She told me that Jim didn't dance. I spoke right up and said to her, "I'll bet I can get him to dance."

When Naomi's eye was healed and we were all sitting on her porch early one morning doing what we did so well (talking), I jumped up and said, "Come on, Jim, let's go into the living room, put some country music on, and dance." I didn't give him the chance to say no. I just took him by the hand, dragged him into the living room, and gave him a quick lesson on how to do the two-step. We danced for a while, and then it was time to teach Naomi and Jim to dance together. He fell in love with dancing.

We all went to a club one evening, the same club where I had taken my lessons, and they really liked the place. As they danced, I couldn't help thinking that it was like watching a young couple falling in love. Jim not only took lessons but became very good at line dancing and would take Naomi out to dance. He even danced with me on several occasions. The three of us started going out every Thursday night to the lessons and then staying for a few hours to dance.

While sitting on their porch one evening, they told me that before I came into their lives, they were just sitting there, getting ready for old age. They had grown children of their own and were great-grandparents, but they said when I came into their lives, they seemed to come alive again and always looked forward to seeing me. Little did they know that I needed them as much as they needed me. I believe in my heart that we all have a child inside of us, and no matter how old we are, we long for the hugs and kisses missing in our lives.

Naomi and I went shopping one day; and as usual, I felt that I was keeping this big secret of my self-abuse, but I really wanted to talk to her and tell her the truth about my scars. I felt very sure that I could tell her just about anything at all, and she would still feel the same about me. When I told her what had happened to me as a young child, she said, "I never would have asked about the scars. Jim and I both thought that you were badly burned, and we thought that if you ever wanted to talk about it, you would."

I told Naomi just how much both she and Jim meant to me and how I didn't want to lose their friendship. She told me with that funny little voice of hers that she and Jim considered me as the child they left behind and had come back to claim me. What a beautiful way to put it. That made my day, and our bond became even stronger. She added, "When we see you come up our driveway, we always know that we are going to do something fun."

Jim was a great photographer and still had his camera but hadn't used it in a very long time because his eyes were getting a little weak. I had taken a photography course at Massasoit Community College a few years before and was beginning to think about opening the photo lab and custom-frame shop. So we grabbed our cameras, and off we went. Every week, we would go somewhere different. It was always the three of us; we went to Fall River one Saturday and shot photos all day long. It just so happened that was the area where they grew up, and they told me that back when they were young, it was all country.

Jim had a small garden behind their house; and because I had grown up in the city and never had a garden, they made sure I was included when they planted and harvested the wonderful tomatoes, peas, and potatoes. We ate so much from his garden, washed but uncooked; it was delicious. The best were the peas because we picked them right out of the pod and popped them into out mouths. They were so sweet, nothing like when I was young and my mother would heat them from a can. I disliked them so much that I always hid them underneath my mashed potatoes so Mom wouldn't realize that I hadn't eaten them.

One day, Naomi wanted me to meet her niece. They were all going to the lake (grandchildren included) for lunch and then back to Naomi and Jim's house later. I thought it would be such fun and immediately agreed to go. When I arrived at the lake, they were all in the water having a ball. I waved hello, and Naomi and her niece started toward me. As I caught a glimpse of her niece's face, my heart started to pump really fast, and I thought I was going to faint. I just froze on the spot where I was standing. Naomi introduced us, and I quickly tried to think of an excuse for why I couldn't stay. I didn't know if her niece knew me or not, but I knew her from my younger days.

I left and, all the way home, prayed that she wouldn't recognize me after all of these years. A couple of weeks passed before I had the courage to bring this up to Naomi. I asked a lot of questions about her niece, and she told me that she was a nurse and where she currently worked. Then I asked, "Did your niece think I looked familiar?" She replied that her niece had not mentioned anything and asked me why I thought she might recognize me. I decided that I needed to speak to Naomi about this once and for all, so I told her that I had recognized her niece as a student nurse who cared for me while I was in the hospital so many years ago. It was weighing on my mind, and so many emotions had resurfaced after seeing her that day at the lake. Naomi thought that it was a good thing, and maybe I should arrange to talk with her about how things were back then. I very quickly refused; I was still trying to bury my past.

As time passed, I could not stop thinking about how much I wanted to talk about that hospital and how much she may have remembered me as a young girl. I was not quite sure if she would end up defending the hospital or admitting how really terrible it was back then. I finally went to Naomi and told her I did want to talk to her niece, and I gave Naomi permission to tell her who I was. Naomi said that when she mentioned me to her niece (also Naomi, but we will refer to her as Little Naomi for the sake of clarity), Little Naomi started to cry, remembering all the young girls at the hospital who were cutting themselves up, putting their hands through windows, ending up in the treatment room being stitched up.

Little Naomi said she would love to talk with me, so we made arrangements to meet. Jim and Naomi dropped me off at her house a few days later. I spent a couple of hours with her, and then Jim and Naomi came back to pick me up. I felt like a little kid, being dropped off at the babysitter's house.

Little Naomi told me that she was very young when she was affiliated with the Boston state hospitals, and it was all very new to her. She could not understand why these young girls were cutting themselves; it made her so very sad and left a lasting impression on her. I talked about the doctor who stitched my leg without numbing it first, his reason being that it would make me think twice before doing it again, and how there were three people in that treatment room that day—myself, the doctor, and the nurse. I hope with all my heart that the nurse knows that I am aware that there was very little she could do back then; she was expected to follow the doctor's orders, no matter what.

Well, I don't have to tell you that Little Naomi and I also turned out to be great friends. I love talking with her; she is a very warm and understanding woman and makes me feel good about myself. She says that she is amazed that I have accomplished so much in my life and that her aunt and uncle talk about me all the time and feel so blessed that I came into their lives. Thank you, Naomi, Jim, and Little Naomi, for making me a part of your lives. You will never know what you have added to my life with your kindness, friendship, and understanding.

Once our strong friendship developed, Little Naomi often stopped over to visit her aunt and uncle and then came by my store to see me.

One day, I started to think about another student nurse who was at the hospital around the same time as Little Naomi. This nurse had me as a case study at that time, and I never forgot the way she treated me; she was so kind. So I got on the phone and called the director of nursing and told her I was an old friend to this nurse and that I was living in a different state and that it has been thirty years since I'd seen or spoken with her. I asked if there was any way she could help me find her. I didn't know if she had ever gotten married, so there wasn't much information I could give the director. She took my phone number and promised to call me back if she could locate her. About three days went by when I got the callback; she told me she was able to go back to the mailing list they kept for reunions. She said that the nurse in question was married but had kept her maiden name, and she gave me her phone number.

I hesitated but then decided to call, and when I got her answering machine, I left her a message. She was kind enough to call back, saying she couldn't believe it was really me. When she asked where I lived and worked, I found out that she was working right up the street. She had grown children and was a grandmother also. She said that she would drop by the store to see me as soon as she could as she was in the process of moving.

About a month went by, and I hadn't heard anything until one night as I was shutting down the processing machines in my store. My back was to the door, and I heard someone come in; I called out, "I'll be right with you!"

I turned around, and there was a slender woman walking toward me. She stood in front of the counter and said, "Connie?"

I said, "Yes," not having any idea who this was.

She said, "It's me, Meriden."

I could not believe my eyes. She looked great. We talked, and she told me that she'd often wondered how I was doing. Then she said that from the looks of it, I had survived my raw deal from those days in the hospital. Meriden asked if I got a lunch break. I laughed and said, "Yes, I own the business, and I shut down for a short time each day and go in the back room for my lunch break."

She said she'd make a point of coming back and joining me. Sure enough, she did come back.

Meriden was one nurse I will never forget. I told her that I was going to be closing the store and moving to Tennessee and asked if she would please keep in touch. While in Tennessee, I started writing this book and in one of my letters, I said I'd like to mention her and that if she had anything to add I would really appreciate it.

Meriden kept her word again and wrote the following to me in a long letter, part of which I quote here:

> Dear Connie!
>
> You were very charming—cute and funny and able to make everyone laugh. A real Irish little leprechaun! Who knew what brought you there. I sure didn't, and you were not one to talk about your family. I was pretty amazed (when we finally met after all of those years) to realize that you still had your mom and sisters around. I guess I thought you were not living with them—or your mom had died before you reached Boston State. Perhaps in another time you would have been a teenage runaway—a street walker at a young age—a young bag lady—who knows? I felt that you were an unhappy teen who needed more love from her Mom, Dad and family, and also some limits. I have no idea what went on with you. It never occurred to me that you were not bright enough to be anything you wanted (and obviously I was right about that). I do remember sitting and listening to you and feeling very upset that you would never tell me anything. I don't recall you sitting and reading or writing—but I think you used to draw and usually had paper and pencil. You were very thin (but I was—so that didn't mean much to me).
>
> One thing I am wondering about—is your family. Every time you talked about them, you make them seem loving and caring

and wonderful—but when I read the stuff you've written and the way I remember you forty plus years ago—you were like a little kid looking for a hug, some affection—not as if you got much love and affection and hugs at home. You seem very close to your sisters now, and that is wonderful—also to be really missing your mom—in a good way—remembering her well. Thank you for staying in touch, Connie, and thank you for sharing, ***Meriden***."

Thank you, Meriden, for remembering and sharing your memories with me!

After three years, I had to close the shop; I was starting to lose money. But I will never regret doing what I did. If I hadn't taken the chance, I would always wonder if I should have reached for it. I still do some custom framing, but it is out of my home, and there is no real overhead involved. That makes a huge difference.

I desperately needed a change and made the move to Tennessee to be near my son and help in any way that I could.

Jim playing out

By the time I got to Tennessee, Jim was playing out wherever he could get a gig. He was scheduled to open at one of the hottest clubs in Nashville, and I had foot surgery. But no matter what, I was not going to miss that night for anything. All Jim could talk about was how great it was to be the opening act for Reese Wynans. For those of you who don't know Reese Wynans, he played keyboard for the late Stevie Ray Vaughan. Every musician has someone they look up to; and for Jim, it was Stevie Ray Vaughan.

When Jim took the stage, I couldn't help thinking that with all of the musical equipment on that stage, there was very little room for the performers. Jim's group did their opening song, and they were great. Then Jim stepped up to the microphone, and in that beautiful soft voice of his, he said, "I had the great pleasure of seeing Stevie Ray Vaughan on thirteen different occasions, and I miss him very much. It's very crowded up here, but let me just tell you how great it feels just standing beside Mr. Wynans's keyboard."

At one point in time, Jim auditioned as a lead guitarist for a country band. They were so impressed with his ability to pick up on every type of music and learn it all so quickly. He went on to work with this group for approximately five years.

I made sure that no matter where Jim played, or with what group, I made it there to see him and be in his corner. I would always take my video camera with me to record his career in the making.

Jim formed his own band in Tennessee called Mike the Cat. It was one hell of a blues band. He worked days at Ruby Tuesdays and spent the rest of his time practicing and arranging gigs for the band. Everyone Jim met was so impressed with what a kind, gentle person he was that they all came out to hear him play. He developed a rather large following.

He started to write his own songs and when I would go to his apartment, we would go into his room (where all of his equipment was set up), and he would play for me. He was using the acoustic guitar he bought after his father passed away, and he said that he never picked it up without thinking of his dad. I would just sit there and listen, and it always brought tears to my eyes. I would remember that little boy of seven, sitting in his room practicing, and neither one of us had any idea that it would all lead to this point.

No one knows just what a musician goes through, but from a mother's point of view, watching Jim grow from a little boy into such a fine young man, I can only say how very proud I am of the man he has become and what he has accomplished.

Jim, you will never know all the pleasure you have brought into my life from the day you were born. You were a gift from heaven and have changed my life forever. I love you, Jim!

I remember back several years when I had a chest x-ray, and the doctor found something suspicious. She wanted to do a needle biopsy. Jim came with me for the procedure, and we were sitting in the room waiting for the doctor to arrive. When the doctor arrived, she started to explain the procedure and all of the risks, which they have to do these days. I looked at Jim, and his face was white as snow. I was so afraid that they would find cancer but realized that I had to be strong for Jim because he was so afraid. I told him that everything would be just fine and not to worry, but he looked so upset.

The doctor wouldn't let Jim come into the procedure room with me, which upset Jim even further, but he was right there when they brought me out. I was told that I had to stay flat on my stomach for three hours and that, again, Jim would have to leave. Jim promised to be back as soon as the time was up. It was the longest three hours of my life; I thought I was going to die of cancer, and my entire life was flooding through my mind. Finally, the doctor came back in, placed a hand on my shoulder, and leaned down to whisper in my ear, "It's not cancer, just a microbacterial infection." I thanked her and as soon as she left the room, I cried like a baby, thanking God for seeing me through this potentially terrible time and extending this beautiful gift we call life.

When Jim came to pick me up and I told him what the doctor had said, I could see the relief in his face. He took me home where I was to rest for the remainder of the day. He stayed close by for the rest of the day. I think he was afraid to leave my side. Again, Jim was there with his company and support.

I was comfortable living in Tennessee, happy to be near Jim and supporting his musical endeavors and making new friends. I started doing some custom framing and planned on going back to school. My one regret is that I was so far away from my mom and from my sisters and their families. The trips back and forth were becoming increasingly difficult.

Chapter Eighteen

In 1994, I decided to take a leap into the future. Not knowing how to type or use a computer, I ventured out and bought one. I had no idea what I was going to do after my purchase but was determined to somehow learn. Computers have fascinated me for years. I knew it would be a challenge for me to figure out, but I'm always up for a challenge—the harder, the better. Perhaps I could become computer literate. Because I had limited educational background and was labeled as dumb, everything in my life became a challenge, and I was always trying to prove myself. When I look back over my life and what I have accomplished, I feel proud—but never completely.

I have to say that the computer was the best investment I ever made. I learned how to type, spell, read, and write through many of the children's programs I bought. By the way, I told everyone that the programs were for my grandchildren—even though I didn't have any grandchildren. The purchase of the computer brought out another quality in me—the passion I have found for writing.

I went back to school and I must admit, I had a horrible time trying to keep up between feeling dumb, being older, and then finding out that I had a form of dyslexia. I let my insecurities once more stand in my way, but the computer gave me heart. It was like getting a second chance to better myself.

When I was younger, I could drive and drive, and it didn't seem to bother me. When I lived in Tennessee, a drive to Boston needed two days of recuperation. But after a while, I was more myself and could drive straight through. One visit was close to my mom's ninety-third birthday, which would be on January 31. I just wished I could take her pain away. Her head and back were very bad; it had a lot to do with the blood flow to her brain and her arthritis. But she always managed to smile.

I had a nineteen-hour drive ahead of me, so I called to let Mary know that I would be getting in very late and asked her to leave some lights on for me. When I walked through her door on December 29, the house was so warm, and the lights from the Christmas tree were bouncing off the living room wall. Mary had made up the couch for me, and it looked like a big Washington bed, just enough to bring me back to my childhood. I put my bags down ever so gently so I wouldn't wake anyone, and I glanced through the dining room toward the kitchen. There, in the doorway of my sister's bedroom, was Mary's head poking out at me. We started to do this little dance, and she came and gave me a huge hug. She is getting so much better at hugging, and her dancing is improving as well!

Of course, Mom was asleep (hopefully with sugarplums dancing in her head), and Mary and I had a cup of tea and talked and laughed until 2:00 a.m. It was great; it's always great to go home. The love that flows from Mary is so empowering; she has no idea what a wonderful, funny person she has become.

I grew up without the love of any grandparents, and I truly missed that. I noticed that when the family arrived at Mom's for any occasion (that particular Christmas included), all thirteen of the grandchildren head straight for my mother. They are filled with big hellos and lots of hugs and kisses. They all know that she loves them dearly. I imagine that Mom missed out on this in the old country and absolutely loves the attention and warmth of this wonderful family. She lights right up when she sees them coming toward her and stretches out her arms to embrace each and every one of them. The love just flows from one to another, and it's a beautiful thing to see.

When I was very young, I remember one of the things that meant the most to me at Christmastime. We would hang our stockings on the wall behind the stove. They weren't fancy stockings like today with your name on it in glitter; they were just old knee-high socks we had worn to school. But we each had one. Mom used to put an apple and orange in the bottom and all the goodies on top. When we reached the fruit, we knew we were at the end of the fun surprises. One Christmas morning, as I rounded the corner into the kitchen, I saw a little white reindeer (with a red nose and a bunch of little lollipops held together with a rubber band) sticking out of the top of my stocking. For some reason, that reindeer and that memory have always stuck with me. One year, a dear friend, who I told the story to along with my son, bought me a small reindeer and put it in my stocking. But the best year was when my son bought a ceramic deer and fastened lollipops around it and put it in my stocking on Christmas morning.

My son, Jim, was on the road that Christmas with a band that was performing in Flagstaff, Arizona. When I received the call that his father had died from a heart attack, I thought, *My god, how am I going to reach him, never mind tell him this news?* Jim loved his dad very much. Well, I finally got Jim on the phone. When I told him what had happened, I felt so bad for him. First, there was a long silence; then I could hear him in the distance, softly weeping to himself. I asked him to please stay on the phone with me and told him to go ahead and cry. How hard it was to tell this to him and not be able to hold and comfort him. It was killing me inside. It was four days before Jim arrived at the airport. I was waiting for him as he came down the stairs, looking so tired and lost. I held out my arms, and we mourned together. Finally, I was able to comfort him and believe me, I did not want to let him go.

One Christmas that I spent at the hospital after hurting myself, my parents came to visit me. They brought gifts with them, and my favorite thing was a pair of fur-lined red leather gloves. When they left that day, I went back to my room, put the gloves on, and cried myself to sleep; I was so happy to have seen them that day, and I loved the gloves.

About three weeks later, a couple of the student nurses got permission from the doctor to take me to the movies. I wore my new red gloves. After the movie when we were driving back to the hospital, I realized I didn't have the gloves with me. But when we got back to the theater, the gloves were gone. I was heartbroken.

A special friend gave me a pair of beautiful fur-lined red gloves several years ago in an attempt to replace the lost ones she knew meant so much to me. I keep them in my dresser drawer, taking them out to put on occasionally, and then back in the drawer they go. I refuse to wear them outside; I am so afraid that I will lose them.

Chapter Nineteen

Recently, my cat has come to mean a great deal to me. I have had many cats in my lifetime but not one like Mazypooh. She was born in Tennessee and now resides in Cape Cod. I picked her out of a litter of kittens, which had just been fixed. All of the little furry bundles were up, walking around and crying. All of a sudden, I looked over to the corner of the room and there she was, all curled up and sound asleep. I asked the person in charge at the shelter to tell me more about this particular kitten. She said, "This kitten never makes a sound." The kitten just looked up at me as if to say, "Please take me home." I couldn't resist!

When Mazypooh was about two months old, she was diagnosed with diabetes. The veterinarian said I had a long road ahead of me and asked if I was ready for what had to be done. I said, "You bet. I love my little Mazypooh."

She was very special. Even the veterinarian fell in love with her. I've had to give her a shot twice a day for two years. During those two years, I thought I was going to lose her; she got so very sick so many times. I would take her to the vet, and he would have to keep her overnight to get her re-regulated on the insulin. Of course, I would start crying, but the vet always reassured me that she was not going to stay at the clinic; he was going to take her home to be with him for the night. He told me how much his wife loved her and said, "She's a keeper." He was so right.

Now, two years older and ten pounds heavier, she is still getting her shot twice a day and still capturing the heart of everyone she meets along the way. She has brought something out in me that only cat lovers would understand. Mazypooh has become a great source of comfort to me, and I am glad she found me.

One day late in February (I was still in Tennessee at this point), I received a short note from Mary along with a picture of Mom. Mary told me just how sick Mom has been with the flu for the past week. In the photograph, Mary had fixed Mom's hair and sat her on the coach in her light blue robe. Mom is waving to me in the picture, but it is apparent that she is weak although she has a smile on her beautiful face. Mom never liked having her picture taken. When I received Mary's note, I too was sick in bed with the flu and bronchitis; it lasted nine days, and I was miserable. I placed Mom's photo on my nightstand so that she would be there, the morning sun shining on her face, when I awoke each day.

Jane, Mom, Mary and Myself

It was March 16, around 7:30 a.m., when my phone rang. I picked it up, and my sister Mary was on the other end. Her voice seemed so far away, more so than usual, and all she said was, "Hello, Connie." The cracking in her soft voice told the story. Mom had passed away. We talked and cried for a while, and she asked if I was going to be okay. She told me that Jane would be calling me soon and that after she finished talking with Jane, she would call me back. When we hung up, I was still in disbelief. I took the phone off the hook; I just couldn't speak to anyone. As I held my mother's photo in my hands, I got down on my knees and placed my thumb over her little hand; it now seemed that she was waving goodbye. I love you, Mom, and will miss you more than you will ever know. You will remain in my heart and prayers forever.

Oh, how hard it must have been for her to see all of those scars on my body. I had tried to cover them up and had only succeeded in keeping a few of them hidden from her over the years. Please, Mom, know that you are not to blame; I did this to myself.

The last time I was home for a visit, I had asked Mom to recite some of the wonderful sayings she had so that I might write them down. She couldn't remember all of the words, but I got most of what she meant. She had such a quick wit about her that we all laughed whenever she came up with something she remembered from the old country. One time, when my niece brought a boyfriend over to meet Mom, he sat on the couch next to her and they were chatting. He had a very large shiny forehead, and my mom stared at him for a moment and then said, "Well, if you don't look just like a newly hatched egg." I thought we would split our sides laughing!

At ninety-three, Mom's hearing was not the best; at times, she could not make out what was said, so she would say whatever it sounded like to her. I was sitting beside her on the couch, she reading the paper; and while I was writing, I looked down at my shirt and noticed that one button was loose. I asked her if she had a needle and thread, and she looked at me and said, "What? Do you want some raisin bread?" I just grabbed her hand and told her I loved her. Mom wanted to know what I had said, so I repeated myself a little louder. She said, "How stupid of me." She always called herself stupid or dumb when she couldn't understand what people were saying to her. There was nothing worse than hearing those words; no one should say them to anyone, even to themselves.

When I was in school, I can remember my teacher saying, "Okay, class, now everyone listen." Well, even when I did listen, there were times when I could not make out what the hell she was saying, and that was because I had a problem with my hearing. But when I raised my hand and asked if she would please repeat what she'd said, she would quickly shut me up by saying, "Listen and pay attention next time." She would never repeat herself. So after a while, I just guessed at what she said. I was usually wrong, all because I was afraid to admit that I really couldn't hear. If only I knew then what I know now, I would have asked so many questions that it would have made her head spin. I would probably have driven her crazy.

I never got the chance to read what I had written for my Mom's ninetieth birthday because we had to cancel her party; she got so sick and never fully recovered after that. So that day of the "raisin bread," I sat down on the couch next to my mom and read this to her:

> You brought five very nice people into the world and watched them grow into fine adults. I can say that with no reluctance because you and Dad were so nice. I thought I would take this

time to let you know, Mom, just how much I love you and to thank you for being there when you could. I guess I was just one of those kids who needed all of your attention. I never stopped to think that the others needed you just as much. Now, being a parent myself, I understand that the job is never done. We give as much as we can and sometimes feel guilty when we can't give more. That doesn't mean we don't love. It's certainly a job I love and will keep forever. There is so much I would love to say, but it would take another ninety years to say it all. So know in your heart that I love you with all of mine. There is one thing I have to say; I believe I can say this on behalf of Jane and myself. If ever there was a greater gift of love, friendship, caring and support given so unconditionally, that gift was given to you, Mom, the day Mary was born. I believe everyone in this room has been touched by that great gift. So thanks, Mary, I'm proud to say you're my big sister. I love this family very much.

All Mom could say was that she wasn't that good of a person. For some reason, she grew up thinking that men get all the glory and women need to take a backseat and are never rewarded for anything good they might have done. Again, this is the way she was brought up (the Irish way).

Chapter Twenty

Now in my life, I love talking to learned people, but I must say most people are fascinated with all I have accomplished in my life. I attribute most of my learning to common sense. I have overcome obstacles in my life and am very proud of the things I have accomplished. Now looking at the person I have become, I can say that I fear nothing, and I walk with my head held high. Life is a journey, and I plan to pick up as much as possible along the way. I don't need someone to tell me they love me; I love myself, and that is where it all begins.

When I think of the value that some people put on material things, I wonder if they really stop and think of what is and what isn't important in their lives. When we are young, for some reason, we feel that we have to own the best car, the best clothes, and the most money. At one time, such things meant something to me as well. Now that I am an older adult, they do not seem important. Looking at what is important to me now, I can truly say that I value the little things in life that bring me happiness and comfort.

When I am on my computer and Mazypooh is sitting on my lap, every now and then, she puts her paw on the keyboard to let me know she is there and needs attention. She will nibble ever so softly on my chin, and her purring makes me calm. As I take a break from my writing, I rest my head in my hands and turn to glance at my mother's photograph. Her smile says that she is proud of me. I think of my son, Jimmy, and know that he has done well and is happy. These are the things that have shaped me into who I am today—a caring, sentimental person who wants to do nothing short of bettering herself for the remainder of her life.

Myself and Mazy

I have just returned from the second hardest trip of my life; I had to make it back to Boston again to watch my beautiful sister Jane and the best brother-in-law you could ever ask for bury their youngest daughter. She battled anorexia and bulimia since she was thirteen and lost her battle at the young age of twenty-nine.

How many more lives are we going to lose to these terrible diseases? I know from firsthand experience that we could be given the moon and the stars, but the deep pain we feel in our souls will never leave us until we can let go. Sometimes it takes a very long time, and sad to say, some of us can't let go, no matter how hard we try. I will miss you, Bonnie, ever so much. I thought at times you were going to make it through the darkness. I know you are now at peace with God.

I remember one doctor trying to convince me in so many words that it might be my mother's fault, and when that didn't work, he went to my sister. Back then, the doctors had no idea what was going on with these young girls, and they wanted so much to solve this mystery of self-abuse that they were willing to place blame wherever they could. That is why today you see so many people blaming their mothers when things go wrong. We forget about the good things that were done for us. "Blame" is not the word we need to use. If we do not open up and talk about how we truly feel, no one will be able to help us to change those feelings and see that we are loved and appreciated.

It was so hard to get my mother to understand that I loved her and felt that nothing I had done was her fault. She had a difficult time saying what she felt because she was brought up within a family where people didn't freely express themselves. We learn by example, and it takes a great deal of time and patience to change the way we view things and the way we react toward others and our own experiences. Have heart and take the time to show how much you care and appreciate those around you. It can change their lives

As I faced the first Thanksgiving without Mom, I found I was having trouble dealing with her being gone. When I tell people that my Mom died at age ninety-three, the first thing they say is, "Well, she lived a long life." Yes, she did have a good long life, but she should still be here because there is a great deal more I wanted to say to her, to thank her for all the trips she made by bus to the hospital to visit me. I can still see myself standing at the barred windows, my eyes locked on the gates at the main entrance, searching for her to come walking toward the hospital. Even at a distance, I could tell it was Mom approaching by the thin little legs.

At ninety-three, my mom was still really alert and on the ball. She would always make us tea, and we would sit and talk. I believe that we had just started to get really close within the last several years of her life. At least, she lived to see my self-abuse stop and saw that life had taken on a whole new meaning for me. I trust that brought her some peace. I still talk to her and tell her every day just how sorry I am that I put her through so much pain all of those years. She probably wondered if I would eventually kill myself with the cutting. What a horrible thing to have to endure with your child. I am so sorry, Mom!

Mom and Bonnie died within two months of each other, and we are all still trying to come to grips with the losses. None of the family is able to think about Mom passing away without also thinking of Bonnie.

Chapter Twenty-One

I moved back to Massachusetts to the beautiful town of Hyannis. My sister Mary has been here for a short time; she sold the house in Milton, Massachusetts, that she shared with Mom. After losing Mom, I felt disconnected living in Tennessee, and Mary suggested I move to Hyannis and stay with her until I decided where I wanted to be and found a place of my own. Jim stayed in Tennessee, but I knew he had his own life to live and dreams to follow, and I didn't want him to get tangled up in my loneliness.

It is still very hard to accept the fact that Mom is really gone. She never complained even though she had a lot of discomfort. At ninety-three, she was a tough little lady and always amazed the doctors with her ability to bounce back. I will always look back during the last few years of her life and be grateful that we had time to talk and laugh together. When we hugged, I felt that she didn't want to let go—almost as if she was trying to make up for lost time. I was too.

July 23, 2001—it was one of the hottest days of the summer. I packed a small lunch, grabbed a lounge chair, and the envelope that contained some pages from my book. I still had a hard time wearing short sleeves because of all my scars but forced myself to don a short-sleeved blouse. I convinced myself that because it was a Monday, not many people would be at the beach. When I arrived, all I could see from the seawall to the water's edge were lots of people's heads. I wish I could explain the feeling that came over me, but I can't and may never be able to. I know I feel ashamed of what I did to myself when I was younger. I stood there, and the battle of feelings began. *Should I turn around and go home, or should I stay?* My eyes searched for a more deserted place on the sand. Against the seawall, I saw a place where I might feel safe. Down the stairs I went, passing all those people. I made a dash for it and sat myself down in my lounge chair. As people walked past, I kept my head down.

Slowly, as I composed myself, I opened the envelope and started going over some of my writing. About an hour into my work, I heard a young man's voice say, "Sorry, I hope I am not bothering you, but I could not help but notice you. Are you a teacher, a secretary? Are you studying or working?"

I answered, "No, I am working on a book that I am writing."

Of course, he asked what the book was about. As my feelings of insecurity resurfaced, I felt like his eyes are all over my body. I could feel the question forming before he had a chance to speak. "What happened to your arms?" I was shaking as I slowly looked up at him. He was sitting there without a shirt on, a bottle of water in one hand and a cigarette in the other, and appeared to be a nice man. I told him I was trying to write a book about self-abuse. He never said a word, just turned his arms over, and showed me his forearms; they were covered with cigarette burns, some of which were fairly new.

He told me his name was John and asked me mine and then went on to tell me that he had been in Vietnam and that he had witnessed lots of men there hurt themselves. John said he'd been in therapy for sixteen years and was doing pretty well until this last Memorial Day. He didn't know what triggered it, but he started burning his arms. Then, with a smile on his face, he asked when the book would be published and said he would love to read it. John then said, "Isn't it ironic that with all the people here on the beach today, I had sat down next to you?" He was very polite and never asked about my scars, but I knew he was well aware of them. As he got up to leave, he turned and said, "Maybe we will meet again, Connie. I will look forward to reading your book and good luck." John, I would like to thank you for making me feel, for a fleeting moment, as free as you were.

After carefully going over parts of my book and myself as a person, I find that with all that wanting for love and affection from a woman, I have reached some conclusions. With a woman, I thought lovemaking brought a common bond into the relationship that would make it last forever like a fairy tale come true. For the longest time, I would not get close to a woman. I thought if I could make a woman happy and fulfill her needs, I would get more love and comfort from her verbally. To have a woman hold me close in her arms, hearing her soft voice saying how much she loved me, was all I needed to hear. When someone is starving for affection as I was, they will do anything to get it.

With my head resting on the soft fold of her arm, entwined as one, we would drift off into a misty, shallow sleep. For me, there was nothing like the touch of a woman holding me. Her hand on my head, running her fingers through my hair as she held me close to her, I would listen to each heartbeat with the rise and fall of her chest as though she was rocking me into a deeper and deeper sleep. When I finally let a woman get close to me, I would sob inside. I would not speak a word; the guilt I was feeling lay so deep within me I could not shake it. I hated every part of my body and being. All I wanted was to quickly cover up my scarred body and curl up in a ball.

Accepting the fact that anyone could love me took me well into adulthood. Sometimes it takes a long time to find the person you really are, and when you start to truly love yourself, then and only then will you begin to see the true meaning of what it means to love someone else.

I have to search way down deep inside of my being to find all the reasons why I abused my body for so many years. I am serenely not that same person today. As I go deeper into my memories, I find a little girl inside me who is lost and feels she is no good, not only because of what was done to her as a young child, but because the abuse continued into her teenage years.

However, the more I search, I find something a lot deeper that I have kept to myself for many years. When I was in my twenties, I did what was expected of me, not only by my family but also by society as a whole: get married and have children. This is the part that people do not understand. I did love my husband, but I was not in love with him. Something was missing deep down inside; and I felt empty, lost, and so alone. Back in the 1950s, being a lesbian was unheard of, and you were condemned for having those thoughts of loving another woman. Now as an older freer woman and with new laws in place, I see how wonderful it is for young people to express their love for one another and be proud of who they are.

I have learned that there are gay men and lesbian women in this world who still feel the need to hide their true feelings from the world. They range from doctors and nurses (who one day may save your life) to lawyers (you might find one defending your life) to teachers (who truly care about your child's education) to politicians (who are trying to make our world a better place in which to live) and to athletes (who play the game with all they have and bring us to our feet, cheering). It is time for the world to wake up and love thy neighbor in reality, not just in speech. God made us one and all, and God doesn't make mistakes! He loves us all and wants us to love ourselves as well.

My schooling experience had, I believe, a great deal to do with how I perceived myself back then. With this in mind, it is my hope that I can reach out to schoolchildren everywhere, speaking to them in groups, and helping them to understand that they are not alone and that there are resources available to them. I know that when you are young, you believe that no one understands you, but you are wrong. I do understand, and there are many other understanding people in this world. You just have to give them a chance and let them into your world.

You never know what is around the next corner, so you must not give up because it could be just the thing that could change your life for the better. Remember, God never closes one door without opening another, so don't keep your back against the door. Let it swing wide open!

Counseling

Let me try to explain just what counseling was like some forty years ago. All that was in my counselor's office was an old iron desk with nothing on it except my open chart, which he glanced at every now and then. When he got frustrated with me because I would not talk, he leaned back and put his feet up on the desk. Two iron chairs that one of the male attendants dragged in from the day hall were there for the patients. The armrests were too thin and very uncomfortable; at times, they were too cold to put my hands on. The chairs were always off balance from being thrown around by the patients. The walls of the room were made of cold gray cinder blocks and were completely bare. The floor, an old black-and-white speckled tile, was more blackened by the dirt left there.

When I think back, I remember looking up at him and all I could see was the cold, cloudy sun trying to shine through the black bars on the window behind his head. He would sit back in his chair with his pipe sticking out between his teeth. The little sun that came through the window would catch his face just right and at times, his face seemed to disappear, which I didn't mind at all!

Every time he asked me a question, he would drop his head and start picking at the bowl of his pipe with a silver tool that had other tools hanging from it. He could not seem to make up his mind about which one he wanted to use, so he would fiddle with all of them. When I think of that pipe of his, it was like watching a bad love affair; he just could not keep it lit! The harder he tried, the more he would get frustrated, finally banging the pipe on the side of the black basket under his desk. Then he would tap the pipe into the palm of his hand and pack it again with new tobacco. He would sit back in his chair once more, trying to light the damn pipe as he slowly started to focus on another question for me, not even remembering the one he asked me before.

Again, I would not answer him. I was waiting because I knew he was not going to be able to keep still. I could hear him sucking on the stem of his pipe, trying so hard to keep it lit; his face was red as a beet. Any fool would know that all he had to do was pack the bowl lightly instead of pushing the tobacco down so tightly into the bowl. See, that is where common sense comes into play, but he didn't have a clue. I believe, for him, having this pipe was completing the image he had in his head of being a psychiatrist.

The stale smoke in the room hung over my head and made me ill; as a matter fact, so did he. The half hour spent with him was cold and unproductive. Most of the time, I left long before the session was over. As I was leaving the office, he would say, "Send the next patient in"—not even a "please." Sure enough, when I went out into the waiting area, they were there, most of them standing and shifting from one foot to another. Those patients were heavily medicated on Thorazine. It looked like an assembly line. The ones sitting in chairs were the saddest. Some had quite a few sessions of electric shock treatment. They would sit with their hands (palms facing up) resting on their laps. They would rock back and forth and always had a dazed look on their faces. Lost is all I could think they were. When I close my eyes and let my mind go back in time, all I can see is that empty look in their eyes. My heart cries out for those little lost lambs that were at the mercy of the fox that was the system. I can't imagine any one of them communicating with any doctor. They were too sick.

That is what I fear when I think of going back into therapy today. But the more I write, the more I realize that I need help trying to deal with old feelings that keep coming up.

Well, I have finally gone back into counseling, and it is quite different from what I expected. When I walked into my new counselor's office, I found it set up more like a living room. The walls were bright, no cinder blocks, and a big stuffed chair sat in one corner. Across the room was a small couch; one could very easily fall asleep there. In between the couch and the chair was a bookcase (one that any good reader would give their right arm to go through). Her desk and chair, on the opposite wall, were surrounded by plants, and lots of toys were there for the children and adults to play with. The skylight made it bright and inviting.

I sat in the stuffed chair, sinking down into it. She sat in the chair at her desk, looking down at me and asking me a few questions. That was when I had the first flashback. I quickly asked her to move over to the couch so we would both be on the same level. I explained what I was feeling and she was very accommodating and said, "If there is anything in here that makes you uncomfortable, please let me know, and I will do my best to change it for you." I finally felt that I had a voice. With those few words, she had made me feel better, and I realized that this was not going to be the way it was so very long ago.

At one session, I started to choke up, and she put a box of tissues in front of me. I held back the tears, and with a big lump in my throat, I asked her never to do that again. I told her I was not going to cry (at least not in front of her). When I sit in front of my computer and write, that's when I let all my feelings out. My computer lets me know when it is time to walk away and take a deep breath.

By taking the time to write this book, I feel I am rebuilding. It has been hard work, but this is my skyscraper to the world with plenty of windows to my soul. We all have dreams, and if they don't all work out, we need to make new dreams and grow in a different direction. I can't go through life regretting what I have done; it is the past and cannot be taken back. But I can take this gift of life and try to make it the best possible life I can live. Love it, nurture it, and watch it grow. We have choices, and we can change our own destiny. The secret is in wanting to change and working at that change. It won't happen overnight, but it can be done and done really well!

We self-abusers are all in the same boat, so let's start rowing together. We know that no one or thing can make us stop; but hopefully, by my writing this book and letting you know that there are others who understand and people you can turn to, you will find the rough waters a little calmer for you.

As I come to the close of my book, you need to know my intent is to try to help others who are suffering silently inside with this disease. By opening up my own ugly wounds, I found the deeper I went into my subconscious, I realized just how sad, lost, and lonely a little girl I was and how badly I wanted to be held. My deep-seated fear of returning to school (which I have always dreamed of doing) has dissipated with counseling. I have completed many wonderful and interesting courses satisfactorily and will continue to take classes that will stir my imagination and spark my interest. Nothing can stop me now!

I truly believe that throughout life, we face turning points and choices that never stop; if they do, then that's the end of all we can achieve. I have many more things I want and expect to achieve in my life, and the choices are endless.

Hopefully, through this book, the television shows, and newspaper articles, we self-abusers will speak out. It is long overdue. We need to pull together and show others that they are not alone. We are not sick; we do not need to be locked away in seclusion rooms in mental institutions. Let's open the doors and open them wide!

The Lonely Road
by Connie Hanagan

The lonely road that seems to have no end,

You search for something as you go round each bend.

You're wishing and hoping as the road unwinds

That you'll find something that brings peace of mind.

It's dark and so lonely, and things are so still;

Your heart feels so heavy; your eyes start to fill.

You're walking that road gazing into space,

Crying out hopefully that it will bring you someplace.

Terrible problems you feel you may have;

If you just stop and think, they're not all that bad.

All you need is a little hope and a little prayer,

Then step off that road and let God take over from there.

My Long Journey throughout the Halls of All These Hospitals

First	Metropolitan State Hospital	Waltham, Massachusetts
Second	Massachusetts Mental Health	Boston, Massachusetts
Third	Boston State Hospital	Boston, Massachusetts
Fourth	Danvers State Hospital	Danvers, Massachusetts

and all the in-between visits to the ER

at the Mass General Hospital, Boston;

the Boston City Hospital; and

the Mass Memorial now known as University Hospital

References

General Self-Harm Information

Covenant House Nineline
1-800-999-9999
A national 24-hour hot line which provides young people in crises with support, assistance and appropriate local referrals. Covenant House also provides homeless and runaway youth with shelter, food, clothing, services and counseling.

Secret Shame Website
http://www.palace.net/~llama/psych/injury.html
a very exhaustive website with practical advice for people in immediate need. It also contains self-help referrals, bulletin boards and chat rooms.

Self-Abuse Finally Ends Alternative Program
(S.A.F.E.)
1-800-DON'T-CUT (366-8288)
The number is an information line (not a hotline) for finding out more about self-harm or admission into the S.A.F.E. Alternative program, located in Oak park, Illinois, S.A.F.E. offers many services including group and individual therapy, in-and-out-patient treatment, and a day hospital.

S.A.F.E. in Canada
(519)-857-7259
A non-profit organization in Ontario that offers long-and-short-term therapy and services, as well as peer counseling and support for self-harming men and women. The program conducts outreach in the form of workshops and speakers.

Bodies Under Siege Listerv
majordomo@majordomo.pobpx.com
to subscribe to this electronic mailing list, send an email to the address and include a phrase "subscribe bus" in the main body of the message. This list

is administered by mental health professionals, and provides support for recovering and current self-injurers.

Support-Group.com
http://www.support-group.com/
A site with hundreds of active bulletin boards and chat rooms, including an ongoing board for self-injurers.

The Cutting Edge
P.O. Box 20819
Cleveland, Oh 44120
A self-injury newsletter. For a copy, send a SASE to the address.

National Women's Health Information Center.
1-800-994-WOMAN
http://www.4woman.org/
A government agency that provides a phone-in and online gateway for women seeking health information. From 9 am to 6 pm ET.

National Domestic Violence Hotline
1-800-799-SAFE (7233)
1-800-787-3224
This hotline offers 24-hour crisis intervention, information about domestic violence, and referrals to local-programs. All calls, are anonymous and answered by trained counselors, and the organization welcomes abusers as well.

Domestic Violence Hotlines & Resources Online
http://www.feminist.org/911/crisis.html
A web page provided by the Feminist Majority Foundation which offers state—and nationally—organized hotline numbers for survivors of domestic violence.

Substance Abuse

National Substance Abuse Hotline
1-800-262-2463
This 24-hour hotline provides immediate crisis intervention for substance abusers, family and friends. Counselors can give referrals to recovery centers and groups, and medical and mental health professionals.

National Clearinghouse for Alcohol and Drug Information
1-800-729-6686
The Clearinghouse hotline is available 24 hours a day and offers information on substance abuse, the effects of individual drugs, and local treatment facilities.

Alcoholics Anonymous
(212)-870-3400
http://www.alcoholics-anonymous.org/
An international 12-step organization for recovering alcoholics. Meeting and local chapter information is provided on both website and at the main (NYC headquarters) number.

The American Anorexia/Bulimia Association, Inc.
(212)-575-6200
Offers information and referrals for people with eating disorders, their friends/family, and health care professionals.

The Healing Woman Foundation
(408)-246-1788
http://www.healingwoman.org/
This non-profit organization publishes bimonthly newsletter for (male and female) survivors of childhood sexual abuse, as well as their supportive friends. The organization stresses recovery through creative and artistic expression.

Incest Survivors Resource Network International
(505)-521-4260
http://www.zianet.com/ISRNI
An organization that provides educational resources for survivors and professionals, affiliated with the Las Cruces Friends (Quaker) Meeting.

National Child Abuse Hotline
1-800-4A-CHILD (422-4453)
This 24-hour hotline provides counseling for children and their families, including abusers.

National Depression Screening Project
1-800-573-4433
By entering their zip code, callers can locate a free and confidential depression screening site in their local area.

National Depressive and Manic-Depressive Association
1-800-82-NDMA (63632)
This organization can send or provide support group information, as well as offer general information about the conditions.

National Institute of Mental Health Online
http://www.nimh.nih.gov./
An extensive and informational website with mental health information and resources maintained by N.I.M.H., the government agency.

Gay/Lesbian/Bisexual/Transgender Concerns

The Gay & Lesbian National Hotline
1-800-THE-GLNH (843-4564)
http://www.glnh.org/
A hotline staffed in the evening which provides crisis intervention, mental health and support group referrals, and peer counseling.

OutYouth
1-800-96-YOUTH (969-6884)
Callers to this national tollfree hotline can reach resources, referrals and crisis intervention for LGBT youth.

Lesbian and Gay Community Centers
New York City: (212)-620-7310
Los Angeles: (323)-993-7400
San Francisco: (415)-703-6150
Chicago: (312)-334-2174

For further reference, I would highly recommend this website:

www.healthyplace.com